Pursuit of Personal Leadership

Also by Dr. Dele Ola

Be a Change Agent:
Leadership in a Time of Exponential Change

Pursuit of Personal Leadership

PRACTICAL PRINCIPLES
OF PERSONAL ACHIEVEMENT

Dr. Dele Ola

The Prowezz Company

Published by The Prowezz Company, Inc.
7 Beddington Street
Winnipeg MB R3Y 0K2, Canada
Email: theprowezzcompany@gmail.com

Edited by Bobbi Beatty of Silver Scroll Services, Calgary, Alberta

Pursuit of Personal Leadership / Dr. Dele Ola First Edition 2022

ISBN
978-1-7779645-0-4 (hardcover)
978-1-7779645-1-1 (paperback)
978-1-7779645-2-8 (e-book)

1. Business & Economics / Leadership
2. Self-Help / Motivational & Inspirational
3. Self-Help / Personal Growth / Success

This book may be purchased in bulk at quantity discounts for corporate, educational, reselling, gifting, or promotional purposes through the author. Kindly visit www.deleola.com or call 1 (204) 421-4018 for more information.

DEDICATION

This book is especially dedicated

To those who would intentionally direct the course of their lives and those in pursuit of personal leadership.

To my family: my wife, Ruth; my daughter, Inioluwa; and my son, Iseoluwa, for trusting me to bring this message of hope to the world. You are my support system.

To those who offered their perspectives on the manuscript: Fred Doern, Remi Adedapo, Tolu Sajobi, and Amos Fatokun.

Contents

INTRODUCTION

The subject of personal leadership, as I present it in this book, is an uncommon theme in mainstream leadership literature. I wrote this book based on the fundamental belief that all human beings share common humanity, but each person has unique hidden abilities that each individual must discover and exploit to live a successful and fulfilling life.

Simply put, the pursuit of personal leadership is using one's latent gifts, talents, and abilities to attain great personal achievement—and more if you so desire. Personal leadership is determining and developing your personal attributes to intentionally direct the course of your life and take responsibility for achieving success in your life. As a matter of principle, the world must make room for a person who has discovered, and has the desire and determination, to develop and exploit their gifts, talents, and abilities to establish themselves in what they have determined to be their exact purpose and calling in life.

Pursuit of personal leadership is a subject we do not learn at school. No number of academic degrees or certificates can substitute for the principles discussed in this book. No amount of soft skills, hard work, or access to physical or financial resources can replace the principles either. Becoming a person of significance—a person who makes strides, stands out, and changes the world—is no walk in the park. The principles of personal achievement are simple and straightforward but require intention, action, and personal courage to follow.

The truth is that nothing of significant value can be acquired at no cost. If something costs you nothing, it was either paid for by someone else or is worthless. Most successful people currently and historically succeeded because they diligently studied at the real school of life: the constant and unrelenting pursuit of personal leadership.

Developing your personal leadership will help you live life to its fullest. The reason we are here on this earth is to make impacts by manifesting our gifts and abilities and to contribute our share to the expansive task of governing and improving humanity. Everyone deserves the opportunity for self-expression and the fulfillment of purpose in this world.

But between discovering one's purpose and fulfilling it are the deliberate choices we make in directing the trajectory of our lives. *We do not become whom life makes us become. We become whom we choose to become.* Those who understand and constantly follow the principles of personal achievement, who are in pursuit of personal leadership, make headway in life. Study the principles in this book, continuously and relentlessly pursue personal leadership, and you will certainly achieve personal greatness and success.

CHAPTER 1

DIVE INTO PERSONAL LEADERSHIP

*In the long run, we shape our lives, and we shape ourselves.
The process never ends until we die. And the choices we make
are ultimately our own responsibility.*

~ Eleanor Roosevelt ~

Everyone can rise above their circumstances and achieve success if they are dedicated to and passionate about what they do.

~ Nelson Mandela ~

One weeknight in August 2020 after completing the work I had planned for the day, I remained seated in my lower-level home office. I was lost in thought. My thoughts took me to several realms as I reflected on my life and the lives of others within and without my circle. Suddenly, an expansive, rich lode of personal possibilities burst into existence. This was no ordinary thinking process; it was a light-bulb moment, a moment of discovery and change and collecting my thoughts, so I could share the treasures I had just unearthed with as many people as possible.

It all started even before that moment. I had been undergoing several days of mental work when on that day, I became overwhelmed with thoughts about my own experiences and personal journey as I strove to learn what had worked for me and what had not. But then I realized that I had come a marked distance from where I had begun. I saw then that I have had many opportunities in my life, such that you may say I have been fortunate. But in reality, no one handed anything to me on a platter of gold.

My reflection continued for many days; in fact, it continued for a season. I began to think deeply about how opportunities, successes, personal achievements, wealth, good health, and other good things of life are disproportionately distributed. In the end, I realized that most of us fall into one of five categories.

The first category includes those who truly want to make their lives count for something significant, who work hard to succeed in their endeavors but somehow still do not have much to show for all their effort. This category of people are generally hardworking and have big dreams but struggle through life while striving to become successful. However, they have yet to determine exactly *what* they need to do to attain achievement, success, and fulfillment in life.

The second category includes those who have done relatively well in their lives or careers but got caught up in the commonplace race of growing up, going to school, getting a job, getting married, raising kids, owning a few things, retiring, and counting the rest of their days. They are generally not motivated to continually push personal boundaries to achieve great successes.

The third category includes those who are notably successful but still feel unfulfilled or sometimes even miserable. They believe there are still missing pieces they can't find or figure out. These people are looking for happiness, peace, hope, personal satisfaction, and fulfillment.

The fourth category includes those who act as bystanders or spectators in the race of life, watching as time flies past without making any impact or deriving any real meaning from life. Perhaps this is their life purpose, or perhaps they just need to know there could be more if they learned the principles.

Last, we have the fifth category: this group includes those who personify success through their life achievements, personal fulfillment, and legacies. They have learned or intuitively discovered the principles of personal leadership.

We all know there is more to life than many of us ever do or achieve. However, only a fraction of people know the formula to break free from an average life and attain significant achievements, successes, and fulfillment. But I use the word, "formula," cautiously as that is part of the problem. There is no particular formula for success. There are no seven or eight steps to success. It is only through many months of self-reflection and thinking about my life map and many other people today and in history that I came to the following seven important conclusions.

1. The definition of success and personal achievement is not universal as success comes in different shapes and sizes for everyone.

2. You attract great achievements and make great impacts not by following some guidelines, rules, or procedures, but by undertaking a process of personal change and imbibing the culture that makes people successful.

3. Generally, everyone has the capacity to learn and grow in the attitudes and attributes of truly successful people.

4. Success is not only about what a person achieves but also about who the person becomes because of the process of reaching for the achievement.

5. The extent of the impact made using a combination of potential ability and the resources and opportunities available is the yardstick of success.

6. Personal fulfillment in life is not a function of what you have or you do not have but rather of what you do with what you have.

7. It is everyone's responsibility to rise up, shape up, and stand out through the pursuit of personal leadership.

To change someone's life forever, just share this rare gem, the secret treasure that changes lives, with them. Read, learn, and share these principles of personal leadership. Almost everyone wants to know the way to success. They spend their lives searching for it or for someone who will share it with them. Yet what we need to do to become who we are meant to be is really no secret at all. It will all become clear as you read this book and discover that the secret was within you all along. However, many are still unable to find it because they look in all the wrong places.

I would like you to follow along and keep an open mind as you read this entire book. I will share what I have learned, experienced, and continue to experience to show you the path to success. We will embark on a journey that will provoke your thought process and incite you to swing into action. This will be a pot of gold that you will treasure for the rest of your life.

But before you continue to read on, go over the seven conclusions again and take a moment to think through each one. Spend some time studying each statement carefully before moving on.

We Each Choose the Course of Our Own Lives

Remember when I said we make deliberate choices in directing the trajectory of our lives? You probably knew that already. However, the challenge for most of us is how to know exactly which direction we should choose. So, here is your simple answer. Your dreams, based on your life's purpose, determine your life's trajectory. I discuss how to discover your life's purpose extensively in this book, so keep reading. Your life's purpose will point you in a certain direction, but you must choose which direction; it is your personal choice.

I too had to make a career choice in my earlier years. A year I will always remember is 2008: that was the year I had to choose between my dream career and my alternative. I graduated from the university in 2004, full of dreams, with a clear idea what my future would look like. I imagined my career, family, associations, achievements, and quality of life. My desire to acquire whatever additional education and training required for me to become a notable researcher in my chosen field of engineering was immense. I wanted to take a frontline position in materials science research and use my talents, skills, and intelligence to make the world a better place. I wanted to develop my innate abilities and become a leader, a noteworthy scientist, and engineer by creating new materials and products and learning to lead teams that would help organizations succeed in product innovation.

So, I focused on my goals and created a plan. However, my plan had a weakness I had not thought of. Something was missing. That something was the possibility of failure or disappointment. I have always been someone who reads and learns a lot about positive thinking. As such, my plan included only seamless transitions from one stage of life to the next, but things did not work out that way. I experienced many disappointments and setbacks that deterred me from achieving what I wanted in exactly the way I had planned. For example, I thought I would begin a new journey by traveling to the West to undertake my graduate studies. Believe me, I had it all planned; I had a sixteen-year plan all drawn up. However, doors continued to shut on me as I tried to achieve that goal. I needed things to line up, but they did not because while trying to secure the right travel documents, I missed many graduate admission opportunities. The whole experience was disappointing and disheartening.

When I seemed to have hit an indestructible wall, I decided to work on my alternative plan: to get a job, any job, and keep moving forward. Success comes with forward movement, not stagnation. In late 2005, after one year of paid voluntary national service, I finally secured interviews with the management consulting giant and global Fortune 500 company, Accenture. And I got the job. It was an illustrious career jumpstart for me after graduating from university. My challenge, however, was that even though I had landed a wonderful job as an alternative, I knew in the depths of my heart that my dream lay in a different direction. Insomuch as I performed well in my job, I just could not forget my sixteen-year plan. My Accenture job did not align with my career dreams. That's not to say it wasn't a respectable job that I was grateful to have; it did offer spectacular work exposure, remuneration, and overseas travel opportunities, not to mention a wonderful work environment and more. It was an enjoyable and convenient alternative to my career dream … but it was still the alternative.

After experiencing a few years of disappointments with my career dream and settling into what seemed like a promising alternative career, in December 2008, the situation changed. In my hand was a ticket to board a different train, to start what I had envisioned starting four years earlier. My original plan to go to graduate school to earn my master's and doctoral degrees in engineering finally panned out. Would I leave my progressing career to start all over again? Should I? Starting over meant significant financial strain, inconvenient relocation, uncertainties, taking chances, and a complete change of direction. My sixteen-year plan suggested that I should have started my journey while I was still single, but I had started a family during my deviation from my plan and needed to factor my young family into the change.

I was at a crossroads. Which direction should I follow? Was it a difficult decision? Yes, by all means. Nevertheless, my dream was more important to me than my alternative career path. I went all out to pursue my dream, to do what I needed to do and follow what I believed to be the direction of my life's purpose. So, I took that bold step. I left my job to head to graduate school, to start a new career all over again. I endured the rigor of studying for master's and doctoral degrees, lived humbly with my young family through the financial strains, and eventually secured my spot among respected researchers in my field. Am I living the dream now? Yes, I am, and I am glad I made that decision, as hard as it was to make.

I faced a hard choice then, just as everyone faces choices from time to time. Some choices may be as simple as changing the direction of one's career as I did, while some may require more significant steps. The truth is that the choices we make, whether small or big, determine the trajectory of our lives. As we make those choices, we must mindfully ensure that our choices move us closer to the destinations we have envisioned based on our life purpose.

> *The choices we make, whether small or big, determine the trajectory of our lives*

And that is the purpose of this book. Drawing from my personal stories and experiences, and what I have learned from many others, I wrote this book to provide a framework to help you choose the right direction for your life and to shed light on what you need to know and do to become an achiever, a person of influence, and someone who multiplies success in your life's endeavors.

What to Expect

This book is a beacon to everyone looking for an answer—an answer to their quest for a complete and fulfilling life—a life full of achievements, successes, and personal significance. You may be a young person just starting out, aspiring to remarkable things in life and looking for a solid foundation for your professional journey and personal life. You may be someone farther along in your journey and looking for fulfillment and personal significance in business or another area of your life. You may be an established leader in the public or private sectors looking to expand your vision and impact. You may be working for a charity, religious organization, or not-for-profit business and still aspiring to become a better agent of change. In fact, you may even be at a crossroads, unsatisfied with where you are and looking to create change, to grow and make your life count for something significant. The good news is the principles of personal achievement are fundamentally applicable irrespective of your stage of life.

As I reflected on my personal journey, I realized modern leadership literature was missing a big piece of the success puzzle: personal identity. The discovery of personal identity becomes integral as we experience rapidly changing demographics around the world and deal with social issues and their impacts on your ability to thrive and succeed. Therefore, I put forth considerable effort to elucidate the need for a personal blueprint for success and how to develop that blueprint. In the book, I focus on helping you cultivate the necessary personal leadership attitudes and discuss how to exploit your creativity. The book also includes not only a framework for discovering and establishing yourself in your life's work, but also how to explore the world of possibilities. It creates context for the seasons we go through while working toward success.

This book culminates in the responsibilities that come with success, including modeling success and leaving a legacy, that we should all embrace as a successful agent of change for society. It is everyone's responsibility to rise above limitations and achieve success in whatever we do through our intentions and deliberate actions. The crux of this book is that directing the course of your life requires self-determination, self-development, and taking self-responsibility, all of which constitute the pursuit of personal leadership. Without the proper understanding and application of the principles of personal leadership, you will find it difficult to achieve remarkable things, become successful in your business or vocation, thrive

Directing the course of your life requires self-determination, self-development, and taking self-responsibility

in a world governed by these principles, live a life of significance, or become an agent of change in society.

The principles discussed in this book are interdependent. You must carefully examine every principle on its own merit but use each one in tandem with all other principles to realize the benefits. Do not isolate one part of this book and use it as a nugget for success. That mistake is common. There is no one simple formula for success. Becoming a successful individual, with personal achievements and a fulfilling life to show for it, requires going through the process, which also requires the determination to follow all the fundamental principles of success.

This process is for you, all of you, irrespective of your geographic location, education level, religion, cultural background, language, political affiliation, or economic situation. The principles hold true everywhere and for everyone. I am calling on you to let us reason together. My intention is to provoke your interest, get you excited, and allow you to make your own choices with every section of this book. Ultimately, I hope you imbibe and grow in the personal leadership culture of achievers. I hope you enjoy your personal leadership development journey as you turn every page of this book.

CHAPTER 1 DISCOVERY QUESTIONS

1. Referring to the beginning of this chapter, to which of the five categories of people do you think you belong? You will need to evaluate yourself based on that category as you read through this book.

2. Which of the seven conclusions on pages five and six stand out for you the most? Why?

3. Was there a time in your life when you made a complete change of direction just as I did with my career? What was your motivation for the change?

4. What major life's decisions are you planning to make now? Write them down. How important are they to you?

5. What are your expectations of this book? Write them down now, so you can evaluate your learning after completing the book.

CHAPTER 2

DISCOVER YOUR PERSONAL IDENTITY

Unless we base our sense of identity upon the truth of who we are, it is impossible to attain true happiness.

~ Brenda Shoshanna ~

Be who you were created to be, and you will set the world on fire.

~ St. Catherine of Sienna ~

C. Robert Jennings interviewed and wrote about an iconic person by the name of Theodor Giesel in a 1965 article published by *The Saturday Evening Post* in 2016.[1] In 1918, at the age of fourteen, Giesel had an unforgettable experience: Theodor Roosevelt came to Springfield, Massachusetts, Giesel's hometown, to address an audience of thousands and present awards to the ten Boy Scouts with record sales of War Bonds.

Theodor Giesel was the last of the ten award-winning boys to receive personal recognition from the former president. Giesel waited anxiously as the president handed out the awards. At last, Giesel found himself alone on stage with President Roosevelt. You can imagine what the young boy expected: his earned award and accolades from his president. But instead of an award, President Roosevelt said, "What is this little boy doing here?"

No, the former president was not just being mean. Someone had mistakenly left Giesel's name off the list, and President Roosevelt had only nine medals. You can imagine Giesel's humiliation as the crowd kept staring at him as he was ushered off the stage. Geisel dreaded public appearances for the rest of his life.

At the age of sixty-one, during Jennings's interview in 1965, Theodor Geisel said, "I can still hear them whispering, 'There's little Teddy Giesel. He tried to get a medal.' And to this day, I keep asking myself, 'What *am* I doing here?'" In his own words, Giesel even said, "I always have the feeling that people will take one look and recognize me as a fraud."

Who was Theodor Geisel? Do you know *The Cat in the Hat*? Oh yes, that was written by Dr. Seuss, otherwise known as Theodor Geisel, now popularly known for his work in children books, cartoons, illustrations, and poetry. He wrote dozens of record best sellers and has been a hero of entertainment in the last century. Throughout his life, Dr. Seuss regularly turned down public appearances due to his fear of audiences because of his singular encounter with humiliation during the incident with President Roosevelt. Dr. Seuss was a notable personality, but he could not get past his humiliating experience in childhood for the rest of his life. It seems he allowed the rest of his life to be defined by his negative experience, something many of us do.

Do you also have a little voice whispering, "What are you doing here?" Dr. Seuss's story is an important lesson for us all. The words spoken to us by others, especially by seemingly powerful people and those we regard as important to us, influence how we see ourselves for a significant portion of our lifetime. Similarly, the identity label society gives us inadvertently becomes the mirror through which we see ourselves. However, logically, we know that what people think or say or the image society projects about you never tells the whole story.

Our society has done serious disservice to us by forcing us to tie our sense of personal importance and potential to make a difference in this world to our background, experience, social identity, and things we either have or do not have. It is much easier for us to believe that a prince will become a king than for us to accept that a throne awaits a slave. We keep asking ourselves what factors are responsible for achieving success, becoming accomplished, and making notable and significant impacts, especially in our careers and businesses.

What people think or say or the image society projects about you never tells the whole story.

In a world where there seems not to be equal opportunities, what chance is there for an average person to thrive, reach heights of personal achievements, earn respect, become successful, make a difference, and live a life of significance and fulfillment? Are there things that impactful, successful, and respected people know that the average person does not? Are there things they do that most others do not? Are there keys to personal achievements, making a difference, and living a life of significance that we do not have?

Well, the answers lie in what I call the pursuit of personal leadership. We will begin the journey to this understanding by looking at the first key, which is the discovery of your personal identity: a critical factor that is easily misunderstood and often overlooked. It begins with asking yourself some hard questions: Who am I? Where did I come from? Why am I here?

Pause for a moment. Take a deep breath. Try to answer those questions.

Without an understanding of personal identity, everyone is lost. Did you know the average person does not know exactly who they are or what they should be doing here? It's not just you.

We all find it frustrating. None of us came in a package with an accompanying manual or instruction book in our hands. We were all born the same; everyone was a little helpless child once. Princes are born in the same way ghetto children are born.

Personal fulfillment becomes a long shot if you do not discover your personal identity. Not knowing, understanding, or appreciating your personal identity can be a serious setback in your journey to personal achievement and success. Most people seek respect and a sense of personal importance, significance, and dignity through everything they do. However, the answers to what they seek still seem far away and out of reach. The growing confusion in the world does not help. The world portrays images of social, political, religious, racial and ethnic, gender, economic, geographic, and physical identity that are counterfeit to the *real* identity of an individual. The common definition of personal identity is therefore only a stereotype, where different labels are given to you just because of your social, biological, economic, or physical characteristics. The fact is that most people believe in the lie and therefore get lost, never realizing who they truly are.

I look around and see many people with great potential to do great things become confused about who they are. This confusion, which I call, "identity misunderstanding," causes people to adopt identities other than who they truly are in their quest to feel important and gain acceptance from others. Our current social environment helps feed our unending hunger to understand our personal identity, causing us to seek personal importance from fashion, social media, affiliations, associations, possessions— even from trying to look or act like someone else by adopting another's way of life.

For example, the fashion industry thrives on the concept of identity misunderstanding. If you do not know or understand who you are, subtle social competition may drive you to spending a fortune on designer clothes, bags, shoes, and jewelry, so you can impress people who probably do not even care about you. There is nothing wrong with fashion and trends—I too buy and wear good-looking designer clothes. However, if you need to wear a certain brand or need to dress in a certain way to feel important, your identity mindset may be distorted.

What about teenagers and young adults trying drugs, alcohol, hooliganism, pornography, and similar outlets? Why is there so much frustration among the rich and famous, who have spent their lives gathering as much as they could but still feel miserable and without a sense of purpose, personal importance, or significance? Why do most people still struggle to feel a sense of belonging as they grapple with the truth about who we are and why we are here? Why do we consistently hear people say, "I have to find myself"?

The subject of personal identity is one that remains confusing to most people. Most materials on self-identity or personal identity have taken psychological, philosophical, and academic viewpoints on the subject, making it even more difficult to answer the fundamental questions with which everyone struggles. For example, the question, "Who am I?" was discussed in an article on personal identity published by *Stanford Encyclopedia of Philosophy*.[2] The answer to the question was thought to be contingent and temporary, where people may define themselves differently from time to time.

Psychology and philosophy have tried to explain personal identity from various perspectives. If you are interested in those academic approaches, you can check the works of John Locke,[3,4] Derek Parfit, and others. However, it is most unfortunate that none of these works can define the human identity decisively or concretely.

In this book, it is not my intention to join in the philosophical debate on personal identity. This is not a book on philosophy by any means. My motivation is simply to get you thinking about salient and relatable truths about your *own* personal identity as you focus on making your life count. I hope to challenge your mindset, clarify your understanding, and help you discover your real identity, the identity of an achiever that can enable others to make a difference and live a life of significance.

The Struggle Is Not Worth It

On your personal leadership journey, to become an achiever, make a difference, and become a significant person, you must first be willing to accept the things you cannot change about yourself. "If you don't like something, change it. If you can't change it, change your attitude." Those are the words of Maya Angelou, a notable American civil rights activist, actress, screenwriter, and author.

You must realize that most of the personal emblems you've packaged together in the form of personal identity have themselves become the source of low self-esteem and are the very things about which we must change our attitude. You must accept your own background, including your physical and biological characteristics, as part of your uniqueness and disallow the things that you have no control over to define who you are.

None of us chose our backgrounds for ourselves. You did not choose the family into which you were born. You did not choose your skin color, your eye color, your race or ethnicity, your place of birth, your height, your sex, and so on. It does not matter if you naturalize in a new country, change your name, adopt a new culture and language, change your hair, or use plastic surgery to change your look, your intrinsic characteristics will be part of you for the rest of your life.

Let me give you a personal example. I was born and raised in West Africa, in the ancient city of Ibadan, Southwest Nigeria, to be precise, to a family of native Yoruba ancestry. You may describe my skin color as brown and my eye color as black. As my life unfolded, I immigrated to Canada and naturalized as a Canadian citizen. When I look at my Canadian passport, I see that my geographic origin speaks loudly. Written in bold letters is my place of birth: "IBADAN." Most of our inherent characteristics, including those I mentioned earlier, speak just as loudly. If you spent the first thirty years of your life in England before moving to the US, your British accent may give you up when you speak whether you want it to or not.

My point is that you do not need to look like anyone else. You do not need to speak like anyone else. You do not need to have what someone else has. Whether you are male or female or other, tall or short, light skinned or dark skinned, born in the Americas or in Asia, born to royalty or to commoners, whatsoever background characteristics you have, you must love, embrace, and ac-

Everyone, irrespective of physical attributes, culture of origin, race, skin color, mother tongue, or family heritage is part of a system colored with beauty and spread across the globe in style. Humanity is beautiful in its variety.

cept in an attitude of gratefulness for the uniqueness that you contribute to humanity. We exist individually and uniquely. Everyone, irrespective of physical attributes, culture of origin, race, skin color, mother tongue, or family heritage is part of a system colored with beauty and spread across the globe in style. Humanity is beautiful in its variety.

You may easily slide down a slippery slope of identity misunderstanding if you base your sense of personal worth and ability to do remarkable things on your background, geographic or racial origin, physical attributes, or society's perception of those. In your mindset must reside the assurance of your uniqueness and a sense of personal worth that is appreciative of your background; this is the self-identity no one can take away from you.

What does this have to do with your pursuit of personal leadership, with becoming an achiever, making a difference, and becoming a person of significance? The truth is that people respect those who are authentic. Being authentic helps you to build confidence in your unique personality and in your talents, abilities, and personal gifts. You are unlikely to attract respect from people if you do not respect yourself. Do not let anyone make you think or feel less than you are. You are unique. You are one in seven billion people on earth.

We Are Uniquely the Same

Our differences and uniqueness only matter when we compare one person to another. However, we all share a humanity common to all people of all languages, races, cultures, skin colors, religious beliefs, political affiliations, genders, and origins. Take a moment to think just one level deeper than the background characteristics I have mentioned. For example, think about yourself one level deeper than your physical body. Trapped inside that body is a personality that, in many ways, shares the same humanity with everyone else.

This idea will help you shape your sense of self-image and allow you to understand that none of those characteristics are primarily responsible for your ability to succeed, make a difference, and live a life of significance and fulfillment. Having the mindset that you are unique and share the same humanity with everyone is important as you prepare to do big things in life. What makes you to stand out is how you think about yourself and the unique abilities you possess.

Although we may not all have equal opportunities to start with—for example, being born into a family where everyone is educated makes you more likely to go to school compared to being born into a family where no one went to school—each one of us has unique abilities or talents we can use to become successful in our own spheres. We can use what we have to become who we should be. I will go into more depth about opportunities in later chapters.

> *What makes you to stand out is how you think about yourself and the unique abilities that you possess.*

Meanwhile, there are factors that equalize your opportunity to achieve success. Let us examine three important ones.

1. Cognitive capacity

Isaac Watts, the hymn writer and theologian, taught us one of life's most profound lessons. Watts said, "Were I so tall to reach the pole, or grasp the ocean with my span, I must be measured by my soul; The mind's the standard of the man."[5] After reading those words repeatedly, I could not help but agree that Isaac Watts gave us the true definition of human identity. The real identity of humankind is the mind. The mind is the seat of our intellect and our capacity to think, the seat of our reasoning, judgment, and memory. The way the mind works—the way people think—defines the person. The mind is the standard of man.

Every human being is given an approximately the same size brain, which controls everything we do, including holding a bank of information and coordinating the thinking process. Aside from the physical and social characteristics of every human, there is the deeper self that has the ability to become aware of, and evaluate, one's own thinking process. This higher-order level of thinking, also simply called self-awareness, is present in every human and has placed everyone on the same level. That is why it is possible for humans to learn how to learn, think about how to think, systematically evaluate alternatives, conduct research, and predetermine outcomes.

Our ability to respond to situations, make changes, influence others, and achieve specific desired outcomes largely depends on how we harness our own thinking capacity and sense of self that we develop from the thinking process. The way we think puts limitations on our ability to succeed and our ability to make a difference. Everyone has the ability to think one way or another. How we think of ourselves is critical to who we become. You cannot assume a self-identity that you have not mentally adopted.

> *How we think of ourselves is critical to who we become. You cannot assume a self-identity that you have not mentally adopted.*

Stephen R. Covey[6] said self-awareness is the reason why humankind has dominion over all things in the world and why they can make significant advances from generation to generation. Our fundamental capacity to think about our very thought process allows us to decide how we want to be perceived by others, who we want to become, what we want to achieve, how we want to make a difference, and what living a life of significance could look like. This fundamental capacity to think determines how you succeed in your personal life, career, or business.

In this context, the self-identity of one who would make a difference and live a life of significance and fulfillment does not depend on their country of origin or adoption, race, skin color, or other similar background characteristics. Your ancestry, aristocracy, dynasty, royalty, or social class is not the determinant of your personal success and your personal ability to make a difference and live a life of significance. Everyone must think and choose for themselves who they want to become and what they want to do with their lives here on earth by paying attention to *how* they think, their thought process, being aware of those, and changing them.

2. Human needs and desires

The factors that determine everyday choices and actions in every human are fundamentally the same, and similarly, the fundamental needs of everyone are the same. Therefore, human needs and desires are generally universal. This concept is not new at all. It is an age-old idea that has been widely studied. For example, Abraham Maslow presented one of the most popular models for describing human needs with his Hierarchy of Needs. This model depicts human needs at five levels, beginning with the most basic to the most advanced. I have listed the five levels below for your reference, starting from the lowest to the highest in the hierarchy.[7]

1. physiological needs: food, shelter, clothing, rest, comfort, reproduction

2. safety needs: safety from physical and social dangers, security
3. social needs: love, family, social group, friendship, belonging
4. self-esteem needs: developing confidence, respect, recognition, status, worth
5. self-actualization needs: success, accomplishment, use of talent and potential

You may be searching for answers at the higher levels of human needs. We all need to have a sense of self-worth. We all need to be respected, admired, and recognized. We all need to live up to our potential, actualize our dreams, use our talents and abilities, make a difference in this world, and live a life of significance.

Although human needs are generally universal, the motivation for each level of needs may be different from person to person. This difference in motivation depends on factors that guide a person's choices and actions; these are your desires. However, the way the person thinks influences his or her desires. The determinant of whether we actualize our dreams or not is our individual desire and resolve to fulfill our dreams.

Nevertheless, deep down in everyone's heart of hearts is a yearning to achieve something important and significant, a craving for a life that is meaningful and impactful. This equalizes every human being on earth.

3. Our ultimate fate

We all live in time in space in history. Everyone has a measure of physical life substantially at the same order of magnitude here on earth. Our time here is limited. We all have twenty-four hours in a day, irrespective of who we are. Everyone lives for a limited amount of time and dies. We are just like flowers that blossom, and then in but a moment, die. We all have a common fate: to live for a limited amount of time. This concept is universal. It is an equalizer.

The amount of time you have to achieve all you have dreamed of and make a difference in this world has no respect for your background or social identity. The concept of time should be a motivating factor for everyone to achieve success. What is the purpose of life if we just appear and disappear? As long as we all operate under the same law of time, everyone has an opportunity to do something meaningful in their lifetime.

The difference between someone who lives to change the world and someone who leaves no trace of significance on earth is not time. We shall dig deeper into what makes a person successful in subsequent chapters. Until then, let's discuss some of the fixed facts about your true identity here.

Your True Identity

If you desire to achieve your goals, accomplish big things, make a difference, and become a person of significance in your lifetime, the following facts must be resident in your mind to the extent that they become engrained in your subconscious. You must accept that these facts are necessary for your personal success. These facts must guide your sense of personal identity and become part of your personal reality.

1. You are original and invaluable

It does not matter how socially, politically, racially, religiously, or intellectually different you are from other people, you are part of humanity. Just like every other human, now and in the past, you have been, by nature, fashioned in a manner consistent with our physical environment and our ability to thrive and dominate in our environment. In reality, we are replicas of humanity, as were those who came before and those who have yet to come. As humans, we are all one family with an incredibly long history. We are all intrinsically copies of the original model of humankind.

You subconsciously carry with you a fundamental inner image of humankind that is authentic, respectable, and priceless, irrespective of any social or physical factors that might have shaped your experiences to date. Your preciousness cannot be valued or exchanged for anything else. You will limit yourself if you do not allow this fact to dominate your understanding. People may not value you if you do not value yourself.

Everyone is priceless. Most people are worth more than they think they are worth.

You must also have a fundamental understanding that every human being has an intrinsic value that is impossible to appraise. In other words, everyone is priceless. This is not a motivational statement but a fact statement. Most people are worth more than they think they are worth. If you desire great achievement, personal success, and a life of fulfillment, you must accept and internalize your personal worth and pricelessness, which in turn provides the confidence needed to thrive in the world.

2. You have purpose and potential

The purpose of a thing is the justification for the existence of that thing. The purpose of a hammer is to drive nails. The purpose of a kitchen knife is to chop food. You do not use a hammer for the same purpose as a kitchen knife. Similarly, vehicles too are designed for specific uses. A sedan is a passenger vehicle. We do not use it for hauling gravel or pulling trailers. Trucks, however, are specifically designed for those purposes. Everything created or invented has a purpose. There is always an original intent for a thing.

If you subject something to a use other than its intended purpose, then you will be misusing it—or perhaps abusing it. It is easy to misuse or abuse something if you do not understand its purpose. That is why you do not try to hammer a nail with a kitchen knife. If everything on earth has been designed and built for an intended purpose, then how are humans any different? There are no true accidental inventions or creations. Humans invent and create as the need arises. Everything has a place and a use, and everything must be in its place and used for its intended purpose. There is a purpose for everything. Even in our universe, every particle occupies a unique space. We need every planet, every star, and every object to stay in their space and continue their unique motions for everything to continue to exist.

In the same vein, we should realize that we occupy unique positions within our environment, and there is a purpose for everyone's existence. We are not here just to occupy space and consume resources. Every human being is here to fulfill a purpose. The reason there is so much misuse and abuse in the world today is due not only to a lack of self-worth but also a lack of purpose.

As part of our pursuit of personal leadership, we must endeavor to discover why we are here. What is your intended purpose? To find your purpose, you first need to start with the belief that life *must* be purpose driven. To make your life count, you must understand and accept that we are here for a reason, whatever that reason may be. That reason is why we, as individuals, exist. We have a purpose in this world, something that, without us, would remain undone. Just as a plant needs sunlight to flourish, our world needs us to flourish. We have a role to play here. The world is waiting for us to carry out our assignment, to fulfill our purpose—the reason we are here. Yes, you too have a purpose to fulfill. I discuss discovering your life's work in more detail in chapter five.

But even once you know your purpose, how can you know you *can* fulfill your purpose? If we are here for a purpose, how do we gain the strength, the ability, and the wherewithal to fulfill that purpose? Surprisingly, the answer is not complicated. Within a fish is the inherent ability to swim. Within an eagle is the inherent ability to fly over mountains and rise above storms. The potential to fulfill a purpose is hardwired in every creation. A seed is a potential tree. A tree is potential furniture. Just as with everything in creation, every human being is also naturally endowed with the potential to fulfill his or her purpose. Discover your potential and you will discover your purpose.

> *We have a purpose in this world, something that, without us, would remain undone. Just as a plant needs sunlight to flourish, our world needs us to flourish.*

Exploring your potential helps you identify your gifts and talents. A potential is a latent ability; it is present and powerful but not yet visible and not yet put into action. When you look within, objectively, to learn more about your potential, you discover the abilities trapped within you; you discover your unique gifts and talents. Putting your gifts and talents into use is *how* you fulfill your purpose. Read on to chapter three to learn more about discovering your gifts and talents and putting them to work for you.

3. You are not who you are not

When you introduce yourself, what do you say? We most often introduce ourselves by expressing what we do or what we have done. For example, you may introduce yourself as a doctor and the director of a department. You may introduce yourself as a teacher, a waiter, a professor, a congressional representative, or a city mayor. You may include your hobbies or accomplishments in your introduction. You may even say that you are a college graduate and mention the name of your alma mater. So, you see the point: we usually identify ourselves by what we do.

As such, the truth is that we introduce ourselves based on the image we want people to see, always ensuring we highlight the positives. What we never hear from people during personal introductions, except perhaps in group therapy, are those things that are horrible, disgraceful, and demeaning. Never will you see someone introduce themselves as a rogue, thief, liar, crook, drug dealer, or so on. And if you were to identify someone else by something of that sort, you would certainly be looking for trouble.

Here is where I'm going with this. You are not what you do. Who you *are* is more important than what you *do*. What you do is only a matter of choice. You could have decided to *do* something else. Instead of being a lawyer, you could have been an engineer. One can choose to be a person

> *You are not who people think you are. You are not who people say you are. You are who you believe and accept that you are.*

of integrity or a criminal. Who you *are* comes before what you *do*. Who you are is superior to what you do. Who you are is an embodiment of your intrinsic value, the way you think, and your potential.

And that leads to another big mistake we all make. We label our identity based on what other people think about us. But people's perception of you does not tell your story and cannot define your identity. You are not who people think you are. You are not who people say you are. You are who you believe and accept that you are. You are not who you are not.

4. You can choose how to express who you are

Formula 1 race cars possess enormous amounts of power to run at incredibly high speeds. They are built to deliver just that: incredibly high speeds. They do so while maintaining spectacular aerodynamic stability even when navigating the sharpest turns. The McLaren MP4/4 is a historic and award-winning Formula 1 car. In 1988, this machine won fifteen out of the season's sixteen Grand Prix races and scored 199 points in the Constructors Championship, approximately three times the points of its runner-up, a Ferrari.[8] How did it do that? The McLaren MP4/4 delivered more than seven hundred brake horsepower (bhp), which was incredibly high for its time. Compare that to the standard two hundred bhp delivered by ordinary cars. More importantly, the McLaren MP4/4 was driven by two of the best drivers in the world: Alain Prost and Ayrton Senna respectively.

Let's look at it another way. Race-car aficionados spend a fortune buying sports cars and driving them on regular roads. Celebrities and the rich use these super machines to flaunt their wealth, yet it is so unfortunate that these super cars used as pleasure cars will always perform below their potential unless owners drive them on a racetrack. Even if your expensive race car *can* run at four hundred kilometers per hour, you must *restrict* your speed to the allowable fifty to one hundred kilometers per hour allowed on our streets or highways.

Each one of us is like that super machine, with the potential to win in the championships of life. However, we tend to drive on roads not built for our purpose—roads that restrict our potential—placing a cap on our possible achievements, successes, and our ability to make a difference. Everyone must determine to rise above the limitations that place a cap on how fast and how far they can run. It is your responsibility to take your super machine off the regular roads with their associated speed limits and on to the racetrack where your potential can be realized.

One's identity story is not complete without considering the roles of our thoughts, our will, and our emotions: the elements that determine our choices and decisions. Humans are the creations with the greatest ability to make choices. Ultimately, we have a choice to make about who we become and what we achieve. Every human being is original, unique, and special. We all have purpose and potential. We all have the ability to dream, develop passions, nurture interests, enhance our gifts and talents, and establish the capacity to become successful, make a difference, and live a life of significance. Not only do humans possess those abilities, they can do so without limits. You have the choice to exercise your liberty to take on your *real* identity as a unique, purposeful member of this society. The process of choosing to become who you are meant to be includes three steps:

1. aligning your thoughts with who you have the potential to become, i.e., what you think about yourself, will become your ultimate reality
2. having the resolve, the willpower, to achieve whatsoever you envision for your life
3. becoming passionate about your own future

To recap, you must self-determine to develop the personal attributes needed for intentionally directing the course of your life and must take self-responsibility for achieving success in life. It all starts with who you believe and accept that you are. Your personal identity is important to what you are trying to achieve. Your background factors—geographic origin, race, language, culture, and so on—do not define who you are. You are unique and loaded with potential particular to you. You are original and invaluable. You have what it takes to become an achiever and a person of influence. Discover your personal identity.

CHAPTER 2 DISCOVERY QUESTIONS

1. Could you list a few factors that influenced the way you saw yourself before reading this chapter? Was there any influence from your family, religion, education, or society on your personal view of yourself?

2. How does the fact that we are all uniquely the same frame your world view in the context of your background and other social identity factors? Does that make you feel more comfortable and confident or more nervous? Why?

3. List three different gifts or talents you are sure you have, whether developed or not.

4. If there is a gift or talent in question three that you have yet to develop, how would you go about developing it? What would you do?

5. How has this chapter helped you reshape your understanding of who you are and why you are here? How would you describe yourself now?

CHAPTER 3

DEVELOP YOUR LIFE'S BLUEPRINT

If I have eight hours to cut down a tree, I will spend the first six hours sharpening my axe.

~ Abraham Lincoln ~

Planning is bringing the future into the present so that you can do something about it now.

~ Alan Lakein ~

In 2008, I had the privilege of visiting one of the most astounding architectural masterpieces in the world while attending Accenture's core-analyst school in Kuala Lumpur, Malaysia. The Petronas Twin Towers are a magnificent landmark, an exquisite piece of gigantic artwork and the pride of the people of Malaysia. The eighty-eight-story Petronas Towers were built in 1998 and stand 1,483 feet (452 meters). Once the tallest building in the world—a record maintained until 2006 before being overtaken by Taipei 101—the Petronas Towers represent six years of construction at a cost of $1.6 billion US.[1]

I was awestruck by the design and the construction materials of this remarkable structure. I had never before seen towers that tall, built exclusively with stainless steel and glass laminates. Inspired by Malaysian Prime Minister Mahathir bin Mohamad's desire to create a structure of excellence identifiably Malaysian, the renowned Argentine architect, César Pelli, designed the towers as an eight-pointed star—as seen from the top—representing unity, harmony, stability, and rationality.[2]

The towers were designed to maximize usable space, with a total area of almost four hundred thousand square meters including free floor space and annexes. One of the most intriguing parts of the design and construction of the Petronas Towers is the foundation: the world's largest, it took about a year to complete, with approximately one hundred and twenty meters of solid foundation in the ground underneath the dense concrete footings.

The Petronas Towers possesses many interesting features too, including thirty-nine high-speed elevators for streamlined function, tapered exterior walls on the upper floors for stability, and glass panels for light and noise filtering. Even many of the interior design works exemplify Malaysia's cultural traditions. The icing on the cake is the observation deck on the eighty-sixth floor. It is an irresistible place for visitors to catch a view of the cityscape and become acquainted with the history of the towers through digital displays.

As I looked through the windows of the Accenture offices on the sixty-sixth floor to catch a glimpse of the cityscape, I was astounded. All the other skyscrapers looked like tiny buildings. I was particularly impressed with the view from the sky bridge on the forty-first and forty-second floors. The sky bridge is a double-decker structure that connects the two towers. Interestingly, the sky bridge does not fully attach to either of the towers to allow for small movements. This prevents the bridge from breaking away from the towers in high winds. The structures supporting the sky bridge, for me, were quite spectacular.

While I took in this one-of-a-kind building, I imagined the depth of thought, the design acumen, the artistry, and the imaginative and visionary mindset of the design team that worked on this incredible project. Architect César Pelli and his team did a fabulous design job. That structure would not be what it is without the design because, of course, before such a magnificent edifice can be constructed, a blueprint or design must always be created first. No one builds a Petronas Twin Towers without a profound and thoughtful design.

That should get people like you and me thinking. Could we really build our lives and set ourselves up for great successes and achievements without a profound and thoughtful blueprint? Developing a personal blueprint is an important part of the pursuit of personal leadership. It is one of the key principles you must follow to determine, deliberately, the trajectory of your life. Just as the Petronas Towers was built with a thought-through design, a person leads a life of success, fulfillment, and significance with a blueprint, not without.

Let's begin at the beginning. A blueprint is a plan that illustrates how to do, develop, construct, achieve, or build some-

> *A person leads a life of success, fulfillment, and significance with a blueprint, not without.*

thing. While it simply refers to a technical drawing in the case of building construction, you too can develop a blueprint for success. To begin, a superior design or blueprint generally includes the following components:

1. It represents the intent or the idea of the owner.
2. It depicts how to do or build something to fulfill specific functions.
3. It is based on clear standards and measurements, which may include industry standards, measuring scales and conventions, and proven methods of presenting plans.

4. It is a practical, flexible, and adaptable plan that can be adjusted as the process of doing or building the thing changes.

5. It makes doing the work, constructing, or building something easier to accomplish than without it.

6. It includes what is needed to develop or build something.

7. The blueprint of a thing is usually unique to that thing and illustrates how the thing would look, including the aesthetics and the attractiveness.

Those attributes of a superior design or blueprint should make you think about yourself. What would your life's blueprint look like? How would you illustrate the journey to your success, personal achievements, and fulfillment in life? What materials would you use to construct your life? What structural elements of life would you use to determine the outcome of your life?

Developing a blueprint will allow you to plan your life and become intentional about how you will make a difference and live a life of significance and fulfillment. A key to success is that personal leadership requires design thinking. There are three structural components of life's blueprint that each one of us must develop as we pursue personal leadership.

On page forty-one is a simple design of a house, with the three structural parts: the foundation, the pillars, and the roof. These three elements form the skeleton of the house, holding the house together and giving it the strength to withstand external forces. This is your basic structure. A structural engineer pays the most attention to these three parts so the entire structure has support. Going forward, we will use the analogy of this house to help you remember what you need to include

Personal leadership requires design thinking.

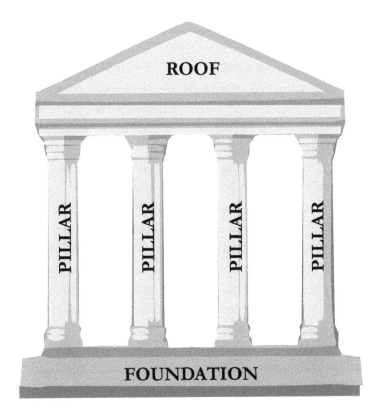

A simple design of a house

in your life's blueprint. These three elements are the basis of the life's blueprint of a successful and fulfilled achiever.

Solid Foundation

Just like the Petronas Twin Towers, the type and size of an edifice will determine the type and size of foundation required and vice versa. A magnificent building will require a magnificent, deep, and strong foundation. A smaller building may require a smaller, shallower foundation. Similarly, the foundation you design in your life's blueprint will determine the extent of your success and personal achievement. The foundation is arguably the most important part of the building. If you get the foundation wrong, the whole building will lack stability and sustainability.

Let us look at it this way. The characteristics of a good foundation include stability, resistance, and strength. The foundation must be strong enough to carry the load of the entire structure. If the foundation is weak in comparison to the building on it, the building will crumble or collapse, either suddenly or in time. The foundation must be stable enough to avoid motion that can destabilize the building, and it needs to be designed to resist the effects of weather, such as wind and water damage.

Given the characteristics of a solid foundation, we can say that our life's blueprint must include a foundation that is strong, stable, and resistant. It must also be consistent with our pursuit of personal leadership. Those who desire to become successful, do remarkable things, make a difference, and live a life of significance must include the following as critical components of the foundation of their life's blueprint.

1. Personal persuasion

To aspire to live a meaningful life, you must have a fundamental belief in your own ability to succeed and make a difference. As discussed in chapter two, "the mind is the standard of man." As part of the foundation of your life, you must believe that your life counts and that you have the ability to make a difference wherever you are, irrespective of your circumstances. Many people through the years have said what can be summed up as, "It is not the mountain we conquer, but ourselves." Even one of the men who conquered Mount Everest believed it. If you have not reached the summit of Everest in your mind, you should not expect to reach it in reality. As part of your personal leadership pursuit, you must constantly remind yourself that you *can* do whatever you have set your mind to do.

In a speech delivered to the students and staff of Barratt Junior High School in Philadelphia in 1967, Dr. Martin Luther King Jr. said, "Number one in your life's blueprint should be a deep belief in your own dignity, in your worth and in your own somebodiness." Knowing your life counts will help you develop the courage to forge ahead in your pursuit of personal leadership. Life is full of challenges, with several mountains to climb, hurdles to jump, and rivers to cross. As the proverbial expression says, "When life gives you lemon, make lemonade."

Knowing your life counts will help you develop the courage to forge ahead in your personal pursuit.

You must develop a sense of personal validation, a personal philosophy that your life counts, as part of your life's blueprint. It is part of the foundation for a successful and fulfilling life. This is not pride or a superiority complex. It is breaking free from low self-image and believing in your innate ability to succeed.

2. Personal purpose

What is your purpose? There are two facts we need to establish. First, as I discussed in chapter two, the purpose of a thing came from the mind of the manufacturer/maker. The product does not determine its purpose by itself. That means you cannot create your purpose by yourself. You are not your own inventor. While it may sound like I have made things complicated, that is not my intention. My intention is simply for you to understand that you do not create your purpose ... you discover it. Discovering your purpose means asking yourself, "Why am I here?" and answering that question.

Second, the purpose of a thing is to fulfill a need outside of that thing. The purpose of an automobile is not to transport itself but to transport others. Your purpose cannot be something self-oriented.

You do not create your purpose ... you discover it.

So, how will you go about discovering your purpose? Assuming there is no instruction book or manual, you could determine what a product is designed to do simply by observing the product itself. For example, a typical pressing iron has a heating element that provides the heat needed for pressing material. The heating element is part of what makes it a pressing iron. However, that does not mean that every object with a heating element is a pressing iron. A hot plate may also have a heating element, but it is used for cooking. What makes the pressing iron a pressing iron is its unique combination of characteristics, such as the heating element, the flat plate-handle configuration, the controls, and the temperature range it attains. It *has* to be used as a pressing iron. So, a pressing iron's purpose is not cooking, even though it has a heating element just like a hot plate.

However, we cannot separate the purpose of a thing from its potential. Everyone is wired—or has the potential—to do something, i.e., fulfill their purpose. This something, or purpose, is a combination of our potential and how/what we think about ourselves. Remember when I mentioned that the mind is the standard of humankind? At the center of everything we accomplish is our mindset. Mindset plus potential equals purpose.

Let us consider the life of one of the greatest heroes of freedom: Nelson Mandela. Mandela spent his entire life fighting against apartheid in South Africa. If I were to tell you that Mandela's life purpose was to fight for freedom, you would probably not argue with me. Yes, Mandela had the potential—the courage, the boldness, the toughness, the knowledge, the inner and physical strength, et cetera—within him to withstand his experiences without breaking. However, he was not born knowing his purpose. The person we know now as Nelson Mandela is the person he became after discovering his purpose. Nelson Mandela began his career in law in South Africa. Had he not become a freedom fighter, he could instead have become the most successful real-estate lawyer in South Africa, had he decided to.

Your purpose is that which you have discovered about yourself and are passionate to develop and are committed to in your mind, so you can accomplish something beyond your "self."

What am I getting at exactly? Just this: the potential we have as human beings is vast. We are endowed with an incredible number of possibilities. The truth is that we discover only a part of those possibilities in our lifetime. So how do you narrow down those possibilities? How do you pinpoint your true purpose? Your purpose is that which you have discovered about yourself *and* are passionate to develop *and* are committed to in your mind, so you can accomplish something beyond your "self." In other words, it is everyone's responsibility to discover their purpose by unearthing their potential and setting their minds to doing it.

Each person's purpose is something that fits in the larger scheme of things. As part of our pursuit of personal leadership, we must realize that we have roles to play in society. We must understand that we cannot make a difference and cannot find fulfillment here on earth until we begin to do that which benefits others. We are made for a purpose greater than us. Just as every part of the body is unique and has a purpose, every one of us was made to help the world function. Your contribution to making the world function properly is your purpose. The discovery of this purpose must be part of the foundation of your life's blueprint.

> *Your contribution to making the world function properly is your purpose.*

3. Personal vision

Where are you going? Where is your journey taking you? Vision is all about using one's imagination to develop a future destination. Success starts in the mind. In fact, visionaries first arrive at the end of their journey before they even begin it. The ability to visualize your destination before beginning your journey is crucial. The truth is that those who have no destination will still arrive somewhere. If you target nothing, you will always hit it. A person pursuing personal leadership must develop a personal vision as part of the foundation of their life's blueprint. Nothing great comes by happenstance. Great achievements are products of great imagination. The Petronas Twin Towers was built with a vision.

Imagination breeds ideas. Take, for example, the title of Sam Adeyemi's book, *Ideas Rule the World*. When we engage our thinking capacity, we create ideas, ideas about what to achieve in life. As the old proverb says, "If you would plant for days, plant flowers. If you would plant for years, plant trees. If you would plant for eternity, plant ideas." Vision comes from the ideas we plant in our minds with our imaginations. Chapter six offers more detail about how to exploit your creative thinking ability.

Envisioning your journey and your destination will enable you to live life deliberately. What difference would you make in your lifetime? What would you accomplish? Can you envision that? When you do, write it down. All of it. Disneyland was the brainchild of Walt Disney. Amazon was the brainchild of Jeff Bezos. The first can opener was the brainchild of Ezra J. Warner. The first commercially feasible incandescent light bulb was the brainchild of Thomas Edison. What is your brainchild? What could you conceive today that could become your reality tomorrow and in the years to come?

4. Personal principles

The universe is governed by fundamental principles. Everything in nature is already set in motion; it is predetermined. Every object in the universe is subject to the governing principles. These principles determine the cycles of natural events. The more humans understand natural principles, the more we can invent a future for ourselves. For example, the discovery of how to generate electricity in the nineteenth century gave birth to electric devices. The discovery of how to harness sunlight gave birth to photovoltaic systems. Humans learned how to convert energy from one form to another and have continued to progress and advance using those understandings and discoveries.

Similarly, successful people employ tested principles of success. No one becomes successful overnight. So the foundation of your life, in your life's blueprint, must include the principles you need to achieve personal success. Take everything you learn as you read this book and include them in your foundation. They are the principles you need to achieve success in your life.

As you create your foundation and include these principles, remember that life is full of causes and effects, where an action has an associated outcome. Understanding the relationship between the basic actions and outcomes of life is paramount. Actions and outcomes can include such things as knowledge and freedom, labor and reward, sowing and reaping, respect and honor, input and output, savings and wealth, et cetera. So, keep that in mind as you go through the principles in your foundation, and ask yourself which of the principles in this book guide success in your area of endeavor? Do you know them? What personal principles will guide your life?

5. Personal values, convictions, and character

Let us use an example to illustrate how important personal values, convictions, and character are on our journey through life. One of the most obvious personal values required of one working to earn respect and make a lasting difference is integrity. Going back to our building design analogy, a durable, long-standing building will have structural integrity. A building with structural integrity will be stable and able to withstand not only its own weight but the weight of outside forces. Similarly, personal integrity makes you stable and able to maintain the right balance in life.

When pursuing personal leadership, your actions must be guided by a set of fundamental beliefs called values. At the foundation of what we do are our core values. Our value system de-termines our responses to life. It is the compass for our morality. What values would you include as part of the foundation in your life's blueprint? Honesty, integrity, respect, commitment, and fairness are examples of personal values. What values do you need to embrace to become successful, make a difference, and live a life of significance and fulfillment?

As humans, we tend to hold on to specific beliefs and view-points as truth. Beliefs are not universal truths. These are our per-sonal convictions. We derive our values not only from our convictions, but also from our experiences and norms. Since con-victions are subjective and can be changed by how we think, then we all have an opportunity to fine-tune our values and align them with our desire to become successful, make a difference, and live a fulfilling life. Therefore, values can be cultivated, and positive values can be developed. We can put ourselves on the pathway to our "true north" and determine the difference between right and wrong through a sound critical-thinking process. The bottom line

> *Our values determine the moral outputs of our lives. These moral outputs become unique to us, and we call the combination, "character."*

here is that we all have the ability to cultivate a positive value system through critical thinking.

Our values determine the moral outputs of our lives. These moral outputs become unique to us, and we call the combination, "character." Our values and character become part of the foun-dation of our lives. What you say or do is a function of who you are inside. A good tree will bear good fruit. The converse is also true: a bad tree will bear bad fruit. Everyone can develop values that can deliver a promise of a life of significance, respect, and honor. At the very foundation of our lives must be the positive values and unquestionable character upon which we build our lives.

Strong Pillars

A pillar's primary function is to support all the components of a building. In developing your life's blueprint, the key question to ask is, "What do I need as the main supporting structures in my pursuit of personal leadership?" For something to be a pillar, it must be critical to your success. What elements will support your building so you can make your life count and become successful in your life's endeavor? Here are the pillars you need to build a life of significance.

1. Your gifts and talents

The fact that everyone is endowed with natural abilities and aptitudes cannot be overemphasized. Yours may not be to compose music like Beethoven, paint like Picasso, or write like Shakespeare. Everyone's gift is unique to them. Gifts and talents determine what we are able to do; they are a critical pillar of success. Think about the successful people you know. They all became successful by using their gifts and talents: Michael Jordon, Serena Williams, Albert Einstein, Michael Jackson, Leonardo da Vinci, Ben Carson, Tiger Woods, Wole Soyinka, Kiichiro Toyoda, and more.

Of course, you could say you are not gifted like those spectacular people. No, you may not have their gifts, but you surely have your own gifts. The responsibility lies within each of us to discover and hone our gifts and talents and make them manifest. Since gifts and talents are natural abilities, you need to ask yourself what you are naturally able to do. What can you do with a reasonable amount of effort that brings significant results, value, and positive impacts to others? You may need to really think hard and dig deep within yourself before you discover you are truly gifted in an area. You must dare to try. Dare to explore your abilities in any way you can think of … safely, of course.

So now the question is, "How do I know what my gifts and talents are?" Rather than overcomplicating it, keep it simple. Think about what comes easily to you. Think about what you like to do, what you're passionate about. Think about what makes you curious and want to learn more about it. For example, when I asked those questions, I came to learn I *am* personally gifted in many areas. One of my gifts is writing, I mean writing a book like this one. I knew I could write with relative ease, and I had a keen interest in it. And while some may struggle with writing or prefer number crunching or find reading and writing boring, I found I could write well. I could engage people with my writing. But most of all, I love writing.

Before I became an author of literary works on leadership, I had written many other materials. Writing leadership books is a gift I did not discover until I was about forty years old, although I had written other things. My first article was a peer-reviewed academic paper published in 2010 in *Philosophical Magazine Letters*, the same journal that has published the works of many notable scientists, including Michael Faraday. In fact, I wrote many articles during my graduate school days, and they helped elevate my standing. My writing gift even came in quite handy when I became first a researcher and then a research center director. I successfully secured many major research grants using my writing gift.

So, how did I start writing leadership books? I discovered another gift: leadership. I am a student of leadership, always learning and growing as I work with people and in systems.

Leadership is my passion, and I continually strive to learn more and to share what I learn. I eventually discovered that I had developed unique and tested perspectives on leadership through my experiences. As a result, I found that these experiences, coupled with my natural ability to write, put me in a position to use my talents for the benefit of others. I had unearthed a gift that created a niche for me; it is a gift with which I can serve humanity.

Your gifts and talents will define your niche and attract people to you. People naturally gravitate toward someone who has discovered and developed and is manifesting their gifts and talents. Yes, people will come to you if you are aware of your gifts and talents and display them. People are always searching for what they need, and if you can fulfill a need, you will attract people to you.

Using your gifts and talents is how you make the world a better place. You make a difference and become a person of significance through your gifts. Your gifts will give you a unique space to occupy in the world. It is a pillar of success for you. If you do not manifest your gifts and talents and use them to benefit others, you rob humanity of your contributions. You deny all of us access to the good fruits of your life. In your life's blueprint must be the plan and desire to consistently discover and deploy your gifts and talents.

People are always searching for what they need, and if you can fulfill a need, you will attract people to you.

2. Your passions

Passion is interwoven with gifts and talents, so it too must be a pillar. In the last section, I said you must desire to discover and deploy your gifts and talents. Note the word "desire." The Oxford

Dictionary says it means, "a strong feeling of wanting to have something or wishing for something to happen."[3] Passion also refers to a strong interest or a strong feeling. Passion and desire are emotional and motivating. When you have discovered something within you worth succeeding at, then you have found something about which to be passionate. Passion drives success. In fact, we may say that most highly successful people in business, art, music, religion, entertainment, sports, et cetera, are people who have a profound desire to use their gifts and talents to achieve a goal.

Passion works like fuel; it is the substance that keeps you active and invigorated on your journey to success. Your passion is your drive for success. Without passion, interests dwindle, and visions disappear into oblivion. The reason you once picked up a skill and then quit after a while was not necessarily because you were not gifted. It may be because you were not passionate.

Without passion, interests dwindle, and visions disappear into oblivion.

Napoleon Hill once said, "Only by finding your own burning desire will you achieve success."[4] You must first develop your passion so you can develop your gifts and talents. Becoming successful requires that you are passionate, that you develop a burning desire to achieve something significant. It's worth repeating that passion is an integral pillar of success.

3. Your plans

This is where you answer the question, "*What* can I do?" Remember, a blueprint is a plan. Developing your blueprint is an act of planning. Your blueprint must include a plan about how you will continuously plan. In my book, *Be a Change Agent:*

Leadership in a Time of Exponential Change, I devoted a section to discussing the fact that planning is invaluable, but plans are expendable. We live in a constantly changing world. The plan you made last year may need to change or be updated to adapt to today's reality. You must constantly decide what to do and how to do it as situations around you evolve.

Pursuing personal leadership requires you to have definitive plans. Your plans must include your vision—your destination—your goals, and the actions you must take to achieve them. Your good intentions are not enough. Nothing will change until you change it. If you want to make a difference in your lifetime, you must plan what difference you want to make, how you will make that difference, and what you need to do to get there.

What can you do today, tomorrow, and the day after toward fulfilling your vision? What is step one,

> *Nothing will change until you change it.*

step two, step three, and so on? No one becomes a person of significance without an action plan. As part of your life's blueprint, you must include the act of continuous planning as one of the pillars of success.

4. The people

Some people debate whether they need other people to succeed or not. Well, it all depends on the size of your dreams. "When your dream is bigger than you are, you only have two choices: give up or get help," or so says John C. Maxwell. If your dream is to serve fifty cups of coffee daily from a small kiosk by the side of the road to passersby, you may do that just fine by yourself. In fact, you do not need anyone else if your dream is to consume the bowl of pasta on the table in front of you. You can do that by yourself. However, if your dream is to build a food chain like McDonald's or Burger King ... well, you know the answer.

The relationships and the level of synergy you can develop with others are essential to your success. Ask Dr. Ben Carson how many other people were with him in the operating room when he separated the Siamese twins in 1987. Ask Tiger Woods how many people and organizations he collaborated with on his journey to success. No one goes on a space expedition alone. Mother Teresa did not build seven hundred homes and orphanages alone. We all need somebody to collaborate with to make big things happen. We cap our ability to succeed when we work solo.

When we expose our vision to the right people, we multiply the vision and set the stage for achieving things we could not achieve alone. One person may be sufficient to lift a light load, but help is needed for heavy lifting. This principle is straightforward. To do great things and achieve things of significance, you need to work with others. When we come together, we multiply both ideas and effort; we increase the capacity to succeed.

Accepting feedback is also part of working with people. Sometimes we receive advice from people who see our blind spots before we see them. Accepting and acting on feedback about our deficiencies, shortcomings, and mistakes may seem hard, but we must become humble and focus on becoming better individuals. At the same time, it is also important to know how to recognize and avoid dream-killers: people who see only defeat instead of success, who do not aspire to anything great and would

> *We cap our ability to succeed when we work solo. When we come together, we multiply both ideas and effort; we increase the capacity to succeed.*

rather you remain as they are. Those pursuing personal leadership must recognize others' negative influences and detach themselves from showstoppers.

Your life's blueprint must include a plan to multiply your success by working with others. Who can you work with as you fulfill your purpose? Who are the people in your inner caucus? How will you convince others to buy into your vision and succeed with you in making a difference in the world? Would you even expose yourself to the scrutiny of those who would help you to get to your destination?

It is true that everyone starts somewhere. In fact, you start with what you have: your purpose and vision, your gifts, the desire to manifest your talents, and the support of others. Expect to learn more about expanding your circle and building a team in chapter seven.

The Roof Is the Object of Your Pursuit

The roof is one of the most important parts of a building. Without the roof, a building is not complete. In fact, you may not call it a house without a roof. The roof in your life's blueprint is the object of your pursuit. What are you going after?

1. Pursue what is worth pursuing

Your pursuit gives your life meaning. One fundamental question to ask yourself in your pursuit is, "Is it really worth it?" As I discussed earlier, the purpose of a thing is to meet a need outside of that thing. The true measure of life is the impact made. If your pursuit does not translate to a positive impact on others, to making the world a better place, then it is time for a thorough review.

What could you do that would be a personal accomplishment for you and *also* be the solution to another's problem? The size of the pursuit does not matter as much as the impact of the pursuit. You may go all out to find solutions to a global problem as the object of your pursuit, whereas someone else may strive to show kindness to the family across the street. It matters not how big or small the object of your pursuit is, as long as you remember what Mike Murdock said, "Your rewards in life are determined by the kinds of problems you are willing to solve for someone."

We all direct our gifts and talents, and our passion, toward achieving different objectives. However, it is not worth pursuing everything. Life is not long enough to pursue every single thing. "But as I looked at everything I had worked so hard to accomplish, it was all so meaningless—like chasing the wind. There was nothing really worthwhile anywhere."[5] That was the pronouncement of King Solomon, arguably the wisest Jewish king, who spent his entire lifetime exploring everything he possibly could.

What value does the object of your pursuit carry? Everyone pursues that upon which they place value. But be wary of the term, "value." If you place value on amassing wealth, if you believe value is monetary, you may spend an entire lifetime acquiring money. Unfortunately, money-getting in itself may not bring fulfillment to the getter. Nor does it solve another's problem or make the world a better place—in and of itself. Money does not have a deeper value. However, using money earned and amassed to achieve a greater good holds deeper value. We do not find fulfillment or satisfaction in our successes until we commit to doing that which is bigger and greater than we are, fulfilling a purpose that is greater. When you reach the end of your life, what will you leave behind as your footprint? Your life's blueprint must include the object of your pursuit, what you will chase after to make a difference and find fulfillment and significance during your lifetime.

2. Finish what you start

The end should be better than the beginning. Make no mistake, the start of a journey is important. However, the end is even more important. Once you know what is worthwhile to pursue, start *and* finish it. Starting and finishing both require careful planning and determination; they require a plan that includes how to start, what steps are involved, and how to finish. Most importantly, include a plan to maintain your desire to get to the finish line. In whatever you do, employ the best of your ability, strength, passion, and willpower to take it from start to finish. If you start a business, continue until you are successful. If you start a new course of study, ensure that you finish. Always keep your eyes on the end, the finish line, in whatsoever you do.

> *We do not win in life because we reached the finish line first, we win because we started and finished.*

There is no reward for abandonment. There is no point dropping out of the school of life. We learn from our experiences, personal effort, and others. When we fail, we learn and continue. When we fall, we learn and rise again. Failure does not equal defeat. Quitting is defeat. We do not win in life because we reached the finish line first, we win because we started and finished. In your life's blueprint must be a plan to start and finish.

3. Stay on track

Staying on track is a challenging task, given all the distractions of this present time. Pursuing personal leadership requires an unwavering focus on the end. Remaining true to you purpose and vision requires personal discipline and commitment. Your blueprint must include a plan to stay on track, to fulfill your purpose. We must center our interests, passion, and effort on our life's purpose and remain determined to pursue whatsoever we set out to achieve. A person who stays on track will develop tenacity and diligence and will be ready to put in the work to fulfill their purpose. You can stay on track now by continuing to read on to chapter five where you'll learn more about staying on track.

The next page includes a complete life's blueprint that represents one pursuing personal leadership. The foundation includes personal persuasion, purpose, vision, principles, and values. Gifts and talents, passions, plans, and people are the pillars. The roof is the object of their personal pursuit. Developing a life's blueprint enables you to visualize how you could construct your life. Living life without a blueprint is like building the Petronas Twin Towers without a design. If you want to become an achiever, do remarkable things, make a difference, live a life of significance, and make your life count, you must develop your life's blueprint.

Designing Your Life's Blueprint

One question that should come to your mind now is, "How do I develop my life's blueprint?" You may be wondering if you should design a bungalow or a two-story house. The answer is not necessarily either. The analogy of a house, as used in this chapter, was simply to describe the various building blocks of a life's blueprint. Yours may resemble a house, or it may take other

A representation of a complete life's blueprint of someone pursuing personal leadership

forms, such as a mind map, a journey line, or even a list of activities. What is most important is that you create a definitive plan to guide you. There is really no specific template for a life's blueprint, but I'll get you started on the right path.

There are certain fundamental questions that you need to answer as you think about your life's blueprint. These include questions such as, "What are you naturally inclined to do well without much effort?" and "If money was not a problem, you had all your expenses covered and had lots of cash in the bank for your future, what would you love to do as a job, pursue as a career, or do as a business?" You can find the whole list of questions at the end of this book. These questions and your answers will shape the design of your blueprint. If you can answer all the questions honestly, you will be far ahead of most people also aspiring to achieve remarkable things. Take some time to think through each question, and if possible, write down your answers. The questions are not arranged in any particular order. If you have written down your answers, then you have the ingredients to start developing a life's blueprint.

Once you have all your answers, we'll start with listing your foundation, pillar, and roof items. Go over the section on building a solid foundation again, then write down five to seven key things you are convinced should form the foundation for your success. You may need to write a statement of personal conviction, describe a vision, identify principles to guide you, and/or write a few value statements. Write down whatever you truly desire to accomplish in the next year, two years, or five years. Try to make your statements specific. For example, write, "I desire to achieve … (a specific vision or destination) by … (a specific date) at … (a specific place)." What is important is that you focus on an area of achievement or a lifetime desire, and then determine what would give you a solid platform for achieving it. Do not worry if what you are writing is not well-organized. Just write things down. All designs start with a rough draft.

Next, write down the gifts, talents, natural abilities, or learned skills you identified while answering the questions in the list of inspirational questions. Those are your pillars. Analyze whether those abilities align with the lifetime desire or area of achievement you have identified. If not, you may need to create alignment.

Then write down two things, areas of life, or activities you are passionate about. These too are pillars. Remember that your passion is the fuel for your achievements. If you are not passionate about the vision you have identified above, you may need to reevaluate your plans. What do you naturally gravitate toward or have natural tendencies toward? Write them down. Again, do they align with your vision?

And now for the roof. Try to identify specific steps you can take to achieve what you desire to do. Create a table with activities in one column, activity completion date in the next, and the physical location of activity completion in another. This table will show you what, when, and where you will definitely accomplish your desire.

Now write down three to five specific people you will definitely work with to accomplish what you have set out to do. Do you think you can do everything you are planning by yourself? If so, reevaluate your blueprint to see if your dream is big enough. In fact, go back to the vision you wrote earlier and re-write it such that when you have accomplished it, you may even surprise yourself. Try to create a vision that you will need others to help you to accomplish. Remember that all you are doing here is just writing down things as you think through your future. Just write down whatever comes to your mind without wondering how the details will work out.

When rewriting your vision, describe how your achievement will create an impact. What specific things will you accomplish and what will that mean for you and those around you? Write down when you will accomplish the vision or desire you identified earlier. Identify possible stumbling blocks on your journey. How will you remove the barriers? Write down a few skills you need to learn or the education you need to acquire to achieve your vision, goal, or target. Where could you go for help? What can you give to others such that the process of giving will open doors for you to access what you need?

Now go over what you have written down. Read your original vision and your rewritten vision. Review the foundation, the pillar, and the roof. Using these three classifications, can you sketch a house similar to the one in this chapter using your own information? Your own pillars may number three or seven. Your foundation may contain four or ten items. Remember that everyone's blueprint is unique to them. This is just an exercise, however. Your final blueprint again does not necessarily need to take the form of a building, as mentioned earlier.

Please note that you can create a blueprint for any size vision. You can develop a blueprint for a sizable vision or project or develop a big plan for your entire lifetime, which can be updated from time to time as things evolve. Or you could assemble a blueprint for a smaller project or shorter timeframe. The underlying message of this chapter is that if you aspire to do something significant, you must have a plan. There must be a design or a blueprint to follow, which may be simple or elaborate.

CHAPTER 3 DISCOVERY QUESTIONS

1. Which one of the five components of a solid foundation of a life's blueprint is the most challenging for you to develop: persuasion, purpose, vision, principles, or values? Why?

2. Did you have any type of blueprint for your success before reading this chapter? If yes, what did it look like? How does it compare to the one you just made?

3. The four pillars are gifts and talents, passion, plans, and people. Which one do you think you should focus on the most given your personal vision for your life? How could you improve in those four areas?

4. What is the one thing worth pursuing for you, the one thing you are willing to spend a substantial part of your life pursuing?

5. Is there something great that you were pursuing in the past but you have abandoned? Why did you abandon it? What would you do differently now after reading this chapter? Remember, failing isn't defeat, quitting is. What can you learn from that experience?

CHAPTER 4

CULTIVATE A PERSONAL LEADERSHIP ATTITUDE

Your attitude, not your aptitude, will determine your altitude.

~ Zig Ziglar ~

The greatest discovery of my generation is that a human being can alter his life by altering his attitudes.

~ William James ~

L et us consider the children's story of three contestants racing horses through the countryside of Kentucky from *The Backyardigans: Horsing Around,* written by Chris Nee and produced in 2007.[1,2] Yes, we can learn from children's stories too. It is not just children that must learn to develop a positive attitude toward learning as we will see later in this chapter.

In the episode, Uniqua is a rodeo stunt rider and "the best cowgirl in the west," or so she introduces herself as. Pablo introduces himself as a jockey and the "best horse rider ever." Uniqua believes in herself, that she is the best horse rider this side of the Mississippi, and that Pablo should know that. Pablo also believes in himself, that he is the best horse rider this side of Mississippi. Therefore, they each think their argument can be simply settled. There is only one way to find out though: a race.

So, they transform the backyard into a stadium for the big race. Uniqua and Pablo guide their horses onto the racetrack, all the while debating who the best rider is. They decide they will race all the way to the Mississippi River, and whoever gets to the river first wins.

Suddenly, they get company: Farmer Tyrone on his donkey, slipping into a stall between Uniqua and Pablo. Tyrone introduces himself and his donkey, Molasses, and tells the racers he heard about the race and wanted to race too. Both Uniqua and Pablo think Molasses is cute but doubt she will beat their horses. Tyrone replies that he and Molasses will just keep going and see what happens.

The race begins and two horses race out of the stalls, but Tyrone and Molasses remain in their stall, even when Uniqua and Pablo leave the stadium singing, *When I Win*. Farmer Tyrone assures his donkey he can begin whenever he is ready. At that, the donkey slowly steps out of his stall. As Tyrone and Molasses continue to make slow forward progress, Tyrone reminds Molasses to, "Just keep on goin!" as he too begins to sing, *When I Win*.

Meanwhile, Uniqua and Pablo continue to debate who the fastest and best rider is. As they race on, the two challenge each other to prove they are the best rider. Tyrone and Molasses are just leaving the stadium, so they think they have plenty of time. So, they continue to dare each other to jump logs and fences and ride one-handed.

Farmer Tyrone watches their antics and reminds Molasses to just keep going. Tyrone and Molasses take the lead then. That reminds Uniqua and Pablo about the race, and they coax their horses into a sprint, passing Tyrone and Molasses in seconds. "Just keep on going, Molasses. Just keep on going," Tyrone says.

It does not take long for Uniqua and Pablo to get distracted again, challenging each other yet again to prove who the highest jumper is. Then they have to decide who the best climber is and agree to get off their horses. It isn't until they notice Tyrone and Molasses have passed the farmyard and overtaken them that they get back on their horses and run past Tyrone again. "Come on, Molasses, just keep on going," Tyrone says again. Now they are all close to the finish line.

The race continues in this fashion until the end is in sight. When, from the top of a mountain, Uniqua and Pablo sight Tyrone and Molasses nearing the finish line, Uniqua just assures Pablo that Farmer Tyrone and Molasses cannot beat them no matter what happens because the donkey is too slow.

At that, the children gallop as fast as they can and catch up with Tyrone and Molasses, who are just a hair away from the finish line. As the children near, Farmer Tyrone reminds Molasses that they are almost to the finish line and to just keep on going. "I think we're going to win," Tyrone tells Molasses. Uniqua and Pablo run up beside them just as Tyrone and Molasses are reaching the finish line. The announcer declares a photo finish. Only the photo can determine the winner, so they all gather around to see.

And Farmer Tyrone and Molasses win by a nose—Molasses's nose. Uniqua and Pablo cannot believe it.

Why would I use this illustration to discuss developing a personal leadership attitude? Well, as the story detailed, Tyrone's attitude was that whatever happened, they would keep on going. Although the odds were against them, both Tyrone and Molasses believed they could win the race despite their slow pace. They maintained a positive attitude toward their race. They focused on the end and did not allow any distraction or discouragement to push them off track. They exhibited great personal leadership through their positive, can-do attitude.

Most accomplished, successful, and notable people and leaders do not always have *superior* talents, skills, or intelligence. In fact, sometimes they are not even as well-endowed with gifts and talents. In spite of this, they still become successful because of their attitude toward themselves, others, and the world around them. As a result, people call them talented, brilliant, outstanding, and excellent. Keep Earl Nightingale's words in mind when you start feeling negative and doubtful: "Successful people come in all shapes and sizes and in widely varying degrees of intelligence, background, and so on, but they all have one thing in common—they expect more good out of life than bad and to succeed more than they fail."[3]

To work on our attitude, we must first turn to our beliefs and convictions; they are deeply rooted in our subconscious minds. The content of our subconscious minds determines our thinking pattern, position, disposition, and feelings. When combined, these become our attitude. And our attitude toward critical aspects of life then determines the outcomes of our lives. This is crucial. Everyone can change their attitude by changing the content of their subconscious minds, by standing at the gateway of their subconscious minds and allowing only things that are good, positive, helpful, progressive, lovely, et cetera, to reside there. In this way, the vision in your subconscious mind will soon become your reality.

When you meet people on their way to becoming successful, you can recognize them by their attitude. What they look like or where they came from is not as important as their attitude. We should always strive to maintain a positive attitude toward every aspect of life. Particularly, we need to remember one is unlikely to become successful if one has not first conceived in their mind *who* they want to become.

Though we should always maintain a positive attitude toward every aspect of life, those pursuing personal leadership and seeking to stand out, become successful, make a difference, and live a life of significance should cultivate a positive attitude in the following areas in particular.

Accept the Inevitable ... Change

Change is one thing we can always, and absolutely, count on. It is the only constant on earth; every other factor is variable. Nothing happens without change. Everything remains status quo without change. Change will always take place whether it leads to an improvement or a worsening. It will happen irrespective or what we do or neglect to do. These characteristics of change make it one of the most important fundamental laws of life. It tells us we must deal with change. We must respond to change. Therefore, our response to change must always begin with our attitude toward change.

If we do not change our attitudes, we cannot change our lives or situations. The change within us drives the change without us.

If we do not change our attitudes, we cannot change our lives or situations. The change within us drives the change without us. To stand out and make a difference, we need to understand that change is the only thing that makes improvement, growth, and success possible. Nothing improves without change. Nothing grows without change. Nothing succeeds without change. Change makes success possible.

We can view change from three broad perspectives:

1. The definite change

Certain aspects of life do not lend themselves to our personal questioning and scrutiny. There are changes that occur beyond our control. These definite changes may be natural or unnatural. Whatever the cause of external change, whether the result of the direct action of someone else or nature or society, we know that situations arise where one does not have direct control over what they experience. This is where attitude determines everything.

For example, the laws of nature have set certain changes in motion in perpetuity: gravity, weather, seasons, aging, death, natural disasters, et cetera. I have found that, as humans, we do not have serious negative attitudes toward changes caused by nature. As much as we dread them or hate them or are afraid of them, we are inclined to accept natural changes and adapt as quickly as practicable. In fact, the laws of nature have formed the basis of human inventions. Most technological advancements we see today were made by people with positive attitudes toward inevitable natural changes who took advantage of the laws of nature such as aerodynamics, magnetic forces, and chemical reactions.

Meanwhile, though unnatural, human-based definite changes such as economic instability, systemic racism, legislative changes, executive decisions, relationship changes, and so on are generally also out of our control, we should learn to approach these changes as we do natural changes. Similarly to how the Wright brothers accepted aerodynamic laws and used them to work against gravity when they invented the first motorized airplane in the world, we must seek to understand our situation and devise ways of turning circumstances into advantages for others and ourselves. For inspiration, one only needs to look to Nelson Mandela, Dr. Martin Luther King, Jr., Rosa Parks, and Malala

Yousafzai, who all adapted to a situation and worked against human-based change to achieve remarkable things. None would call themselves spectacular people, but they achieved spectacular things.

Unless you change your attitude toward things outside of your control, you will continue to suffer the consequences of change. This does not mean that accepting definite change will keep it from being an unpleasant experience, only that we have an ability to choose our response and consequent actions to whatever situations we face.

The true measure of the impact of any definite change that is external and not within the control of an individual is the extent of adjustment or adaptation required to normalize the impact. This required adaptation becomes a continuous activity due to the constant nature of change. As we adapt to one change, so do we experience change in other areas. In other words, we have only one option when it comes to change. We must develop our attitude to include the willpower to accept the change, modify our plans, take alternative action, and adapt to the change.

Every change presents an opportunity for creativity. To stand out, become successful, and make a difference, we need to maintain a positive attitude toward definite change and use different avenues to turn the situation around, to turn a negative into a positive for ourselves and others.

2. The changeable change

Most people naturally adopt an attitude of blaming someone else for changes they allowed to happen. Yet if something is not moving in the direction you want it to, you can change course direction by changing your actions. We can change change. You are not entitled to blame anyone else for your failed career, moribund business, unruly children, unhappiness, lack of success, bad relationships, or lost opportunities.

If you cannot blame someone else, then you cannot be a victim of the circumstances either. Instead of waiting for life to happen to you, you can take control of your circumstances by first controlling your attitude and then taking actions toward forestalling your own future.

As part of your effort to stand out, to become successful, and live a fulfilling life, you must take personal responsibility for whatsoever situation you find yourself in and take action to create change, thereby improving your situation. If something is not working out the way you had envisioned or planned, or an external situation is working against your plan, you have the choice to either do nothing and allow the circumstances to overtake you or to step forward, change the change, and create the experience you want.

3. The needed change

The ideal life you are envisioning does not already exist. You must create it. If you want to see a particular change in the world, go ahead and create the change. Most great achievers and successful people see what others do not see and act to make it reality. Good things result from positive change made by people with positive attitudes.

> *The ideal life you are envisioning does not already exist. You must create it. If you want to see a particular change in the world, go ahead and create the change.*

Opportunities to achieve remarkable things and become agents of change are available to everyone. To lead change, you must start with your own gifts, talents, and abilities. What do you have today that you can use to create a new future for yourself and others around you? The world needs change agents to bring about the needed change in our families, politics, economics, human rights, technology, healthcare, laws, entertainment, sports, religion, and more. The options and positive results of a positive attitude toward change are endless.

Focus on Value, Not Personal Gain

We all have to evaluate why we want the success we are looking for. What is the overarching benefit of the success you are spending your entire lifetime pursuing? What are you trying to achieve by becoming successful in this way? As I discussed in the previous chapters, the purpose of a thing is to fulfill a need outside the thing itself. The overall purpose of your success in life is unlikely to be the amassing of material possessions, living in the most expensive house, driving the most exotic car, going on the most expensive vacation, and having every pleasurable thing at your beck and call.

Financial and material wealth are, in many cases, the byproducts of fulfilling our purpose in life. We attract good things when we fulfill our purpose, but we should be careful not to be entrapped by putting self-aggrandizement center stage. If we define success by riches, possessions, and fame, then we undermine the invaluable contributions of leaders who have achieved enormous success, fulfilled purpose, and made the world a better place yet did not amass such wealth, much like Mother Theresa.

Why is this important? Mark Hughes, founder and pastor of the Church of the Rock in Winnipeg, Manitoba, explains why using his experience attending and officiating funeral services. According to Hughes, family members, friends, and associates rarely remember the deceased for their material possessions: cars, houses, boats, and assets. Instead, they are remembered for their relationships, deeds, and the impacts they made in the lives of others. Have you ever given deep thought to what you will be remembered for?

The pursuit of personal leadership requires adding value to people, which leads to being remembered for doing exactly that. We shall discuss leaving a legacy in greater detail in chapter ten. Needless to say, a successful person's attitude must be focused on creating and delivering value to humanity. The more resources you acquire from your success, the more the responsibility for value creation and value adding rests on your shoulders. Real achievers and successful people do not use people to amass resources unto themselves; they use resources to add value to people and improve society.

> *Real achievers and successful people do not use people to amass resources unto themselves; they use resources to add value to people and improve society.*

Continually Pursue Knowledge

One of the most powerful human activities on earth is applying what we know and what we've learned. Knowledge is powerful. Knowledge empowers people to become free. We fail when we lack knowledge. You do not know what you do not know. I have long been fascinated by this line in the Book of Proverbs: "The labor of a fool so wearies him [because he is ignorant] that he does not even know how to go to a city."[4] As harsh as that may sound, it is true.

If you want to succeed in something, you cannot afford to be ignorant in that area. The result of ignorance is weariness and frustration. Ignorance makes people keep doing the same thing the same way yet expecting a different result. "The person who stops studying merely because he has finished school is forever hopelessly doomed to mediocrity, no matter what may be his calling. The way of success is the way of continuous pursuit of knowledge," said Napoleon Hill. Knowledge allows us to devise more than one way of doing something. Knowledge allows us to explore options for success. In fact, knowledge will show you *how* to be successful.

The challenge for most of us is that we do not continue learning. Consequently, we do not solve problems, and we are unable to improve our lives. Continuous learning is an attitude we must practice. Saying or thinking that something is new is a myth. There is nothing new. No matter what you plan to succeed in, you will eventually find there were people before you who attempted or accomplished something similar.

For example, the greatest scientific discoveries were made on foundations already laid by previous scientists. If you intend to be a great scientist, you must be ready to learn what has been done before you. Otherwise, you will simply reinvent the wheel. Even if your goal is to achieve something novel and spectacular in your field, you still have an opportunity for a head start by learning what has already been done.

Fortunately, we all have several avenues to acquiring knowledge available, especially in this age of readily accessible information and data. In most cases, the information you need for success already exists in books, archives, journals, magazines, articles, blogs, podcasts, and more. You can learn directly from people who have already been successful—and those who have failed—in the area of your life endeavor.

Sir Isaac Newton, in his 1675 letter to Robert Hook, said, "If I see further, it is by standing on the shoulders of giants."[5] If you try to learn from your own experiences alone, you will need a whole lifetime to start any endeavor. Every one of us has the opportunity to stand on the shoulders of giants. We do that by learning from the experiences of others.

Meanwhile, knowledge itself is not enough. As I mentioned earlier, one of the most powerful activities on earth is applying knowledge. The power of knowledge lies in its application, in the analyzing, synthesizing, and improving of things and circumstances. Knowledge becomes powerful when we develop an action plan for its use.

To apply knowledge, we need to first understand what we have learned. Knowledge is the acquisition of information and facts. Understanding is the comprehension of the information we acquired. It is a higher level of learning. Understanding requires thinking logically about information and facts. A person that understands something has grasped its essence and can interpret what was learned. Understanding sets the stage for analyzing and applying what we learn. Without understanding, we remain at the level of head knowledge: the lowest level of learning.

People that have attained significant personal leadership have a positive attitude toward learning. They fill their subconscious minds with content that enables them to be successful and draw from the richness of their knowledge as they approach the affairs of life. We can all fill our subconscious minds with content through meditation, which is the thinking and rethinking of what enters our minds. When we think and rethink, or meditate, on what we learn, we begin to develop context for using the knowledge. We then fill our subconscious mind with content we need to respond to the affairs of life. In this way, the knowledge we have disseminated during meditation becomes engrained in our subconscious minds, and this determines the pattern of our thinking. This pattern of thinking determines the direction of our lives.

We must stand at the gateway of our own minds, judiciously selecting the content that fills our subconscious minds. In other words, we must guard our thoughts to guard our subconscious minds. What you allow into your subconscious mind determines your response to life. If you allow garbage in, only garbage will come out. If you dwell and meditate on impossibilities, failure is imminent for you. But if your subconscious mind is full of possibilities and positive thoughts, coupled with the will and passion to succeed, you will find yourself on the right track.

> *What you allow into your subconscious mind determines your response to life.*

Nevertheless, using knowledge to create what we want to see in our daily lives is called wisdom. Wisdom is principal. Wisdom is the good judgment and the intelligence we use in making decisions based on the knowledge we have learned. Successful people are wise. We make our lives count using wisdom. We need wisdom to build successful businesses, families, governments, and the society. More importantly, we use knowledge to improve situations and add value to others and ourselves through wisdom.

Work to Achieve Change

Work has no substitute. Those who understand and exploit both the purpose and the secret of work discover treasures. Yes, I said treasures. Treasures do not have to be material. The treasures are in the change you make, in the achievements you gain, and in the betterment of society. I know it is easy to struggle with the idea that so many people around us work hard but are still not as successful as we would expect. If we were to measure the success of an individual by the amount of work done, then the person that works harder or does more work should be more successful, happier, and more fulfilled. However, we know that is not true. Simply working to work is not the same as working to achieve change.

To live a successful and meaningful life, we must first understand the purpose of work. Why do we have to work? Work is the means through which we create and/or change things. Nothing changes until we do work. Work is the means of converting raw potatoes into cooked mashed potatoes, whether with physical human effort or with a machine. Nothing changes until we change it through work.

Every element of nature has energy. The purpose of energy is to do work. Do you possess energy? Of course you do. So work. Only those who give themselves over to work for change deserve things of substance. We can only improve our own and other's situations with work. We change the world through what we do. We cannot expect results where we have not contributed effort. There can be no harvest without sowing. Life gives back to us, amplified, whatever we give to life through work. Work is a primary principle of life. The pursuit of personal leadership necessitates work. Work is not a burden to those with a resolve to make a difference and change the world. Work is the means through which we improve our lives.

> *We can only improve our own and other's situations with work. We change the world through what we do.*

Let us flash back to the previous chapter where I discussed the need for a life's blueprint. Designing your blueprint is not enough; you cannot stop there, or you will achieve nothing. You must implement your blueprint, and the way to do that is by getting to work. Work is rewarding when it is done according to a plan, design, or blueprint. This suggests that energy—and work—can be wasted if not appropriately directed and explains why many people work without much result to show for their work. They are not working to achieve change. They are not working with a plan. Working hard is good, but working smart is even better. You do not have an unlimited capacity to work. Therefore, guide your work with a plan. Expend your energy on what gets you closer to your destination.

Become an Overcomer

There are five ways to conquer a mountain but only four that are effective: you can climb it, tunnel through it, dig below it, or re-move it. The fifth way is to go around it, to avoid it. That may be the easiest way too, but you will get nothing in return for going around it. Life is full of challenges, but they exist so they can be overcome. A landscape where great achievements are made is not a level field. It is a landscape full of obstacles and barriers. If you have a mountain in your way, you need to conquer it. A successful person has a positive attitude toward removing obstacles, an attitude conducive to breaking barriers.

If your victory is at the top of the mountain, then climb the mountain. Do not be afraid or lazy. There is always a price to pay to reach the summit, but nothing equates to

A landscape where great achievements are made is not a level field. It is a landscape full of obstacles and barriers

the achievement found on the mountaintop. No one finds themselves on the top of the mountain because they drifted onto it. Climbing a mountain is difficult but worth it. If you keep your eyes on the prize at the top, paying the price to get there becomes a doable task.

One of the greatest attributes of achievers is that they are consistently persistent. They do not give up in the face of difficulty and adversity. To make strides, become successful, and make a difference, we must develop the mindset of an overcomer. Then we can climb the mountain, cross the river, jump the hurdle, and navigate the complex landscape of life. We must maintain a positive can-do attitude when the going gets tough.

Develop Self-Motivation and Self-Accountability

You have probably heard that life is a marathon, not a sprint. Yes, it is true that it is not how fast we achieve that matters but how well we achieve. However, life is still a race. Time is not on our side. We still have to do what we have to do while we are still able to do it. The clock of life keeps ticking. Our time here is not as abundant as we usually imagine. If your attitude to your own tasks is that work is burdensome, you will only play a waiting game, engaging in dilly-dallying and dragging your feet, thereby forming a habit of not starting or not completing work. Whatever you need to do, do it. Allow no room for procrastination. Do not push what you can do today to tomorrow. The only way to take care of tomorrow is by doing something today.

If you want your life to count, then you need to develop a habit of motivating yourself into action and becoming self-accountable for this habit. Brian Tracy, when discussing the concept of positive addiction in his book, *Eat that Frog*, said,

> One of the keys to your living a wonderful life, having a successful career, and feeling terrific about yourself is to develop the habit of starting and finishing important jobs. When you

do, this behavior will take on a power of its own and you'll find it easier to complete important tasks than not to complete them.[6]

A self-motivated individual wakes up and faces their tasks every day, driven by their desire and determination to succeed and without the need for external motivation. Self-motivation requires independent thinking, personal awareness, and personal drive for success.

Overcoming procrastination also requires self-accountability. Hold yourself accountable by forming a habit of starting and completing tasks. You are unlikely to be always under pressure to succeed, and no one else will hold you accountable or prevent you from procrastinating. Be true to yourself and your end goal.

The key here is to develop an attitude of self-motivation and self-accountability. Do not think others will give you motivation. Your dreams should keep you focused on your tasks and activities without external motivation. Your attitude to completing the tasks necessary to achieve your own success should be that of expediency, which requires self-motivation and self-accountability.

Keep Riding the Rollercoaster

A person of substance and value, who stands out and makes a difference, needs to maintain an attitude of doing whatever it takes to become successful. The success of yesterday does not guarantee the success of today. When you are on a rollercoaster, remember that it does not last forever. Enjoy the ride but remember that as you crest the lift hill and plummet to the ground,

The success of yesterday does not guarantee the success of today.

so do you need to begin another climb. In fact, most successful people are usually habitually successful, and it starts as an attitude.

This may sound counterintuitive, but it is not. Success has a way of getting in the way of success. For example, if you set a goal of making a million dollars yearly in your business and you achieve that goal, you may become complacent and remain at that level of success unless you set a bigger goal. Should not becoming successful always make us become more successful? Not necessarily. It depends on your thoughts, feelings, and disposition—or your attitude—toward success. If you see success as a destination, you may not be motivated to initiate the next action that catapults you to the next success. It is important to feel happy, celebrate, and enjoy the sense of accomplishment that comes with completing something, whether big or small. However, it is equally important to remind ourselves that our destination is not an end but a continuous journey.

Attitude Wrap-up: The Man with an Exemplary Attitude

Let us wrap up this chapter by talking briefly about Paul Alexander: the man in the iron lung.[7] Paul was six years old when he contracted polio during the 1952 outbreak that ravaged Texas. His body ended up encased in a metal canister, the iron lung, just like numerous other children. Infected children died in large numbers daily during those times.

Paul is one of the survivors. He recovered from the polio infection but was left almost completely paralyzed from the neck down. His diaphragm could no longer support him though, so he continued to need the iron lung. However, living with an iron lung was torturous. Paul needed to lay flat on his back with his head on a pillow while his entire body from the neck down was encased in the metal cylinder. The pressure differential induced in the machine cyclically inflated and deflated his lungs, essentially breathing for him. Paul needed to remain in the iron lung to live.

The most integral pillar of Paul's experience was his resolve to live. He clearly remembered times in the hospital wards when doctors on their rounds would say, "He's going to die today," or "He shouldn't be alive." This infuriated Paul and made him *want* to live. He could have chosen either life or death. But his attitude toward life, motivation, and work incited him to decide to live.

A few years later, with support from his therapist, Mrs. Sullivan, Paul learned to push some air down his vocal cords and into his lungs in a process he called "frog breathing." After a year of practice, he learned to frog-breathe for up to three minutes. He soon got better at it and was able to frog-breathe reliably for long enough to spend short periods outside the iron lung. Eventually, he worked hard enough that he could spend more time outside, though he still needed to sleep in the iron lung as he needed to be awake to frog-breath.

Paul, at 21, became the first person to graduate from a Dallas high school without physically attending a class. He later attended Southern Methodist University in Dallas and then the law school at the University of Texas at Austin. Paul went on to practice law in Dallas and Fort Worth for decades despite his physical condition. He made his court appearances in a wheelchair that supported his body in an upright position. But Paul did not see himself as someone with a handicap. He flew in airplanes, visited clubs, saw the ocean, prayed in church, and fell in love. What an attitude to life!

Now seventy-five as of this writing, Paul is once again confined to the iron lung full time, not having been out of the machine for more than five minutes in years. No one has ever used the iron lung for so long. Paul still writes by using his mouth to manipulate a foot-long stick with a pen attached to the end. For Paul, the journey of life is far from easy as he manages his deteriorating health.

> *The difference between someone who lives to make a difference and someone who lives for mediocrity is the attitude of the mind.*

But there is a remarkable lesson about attitude to learn from Paul. If he could achieve so much despite his experience, you and I have no excuse. Paul's story is a clear example that the difference between someone who lives to make a difference and someone who lives for mediocrity is the attitude of the mind. A person is exactly what he or she thinks.

CHAPTER 4 DISCOVERY QUESTIONS

1. Knowing that our beliefs and convictions, and consequently our attitudes to life, are deeply rooted in the content of our subconscious minds, how do you think you can control the content of your subconscious mind? Why is this important?

2. In this chapter, you read about definite change, changeable change, and needed change. Could you identify one needed change you are capable of bringing to the world either as an individual or by working with others?

3. Our attitude to knowledge should be that of continuous learning. List three areas of knowledge you must improve as part of your pursuit of personal leadership. Where and how would you acquire the knowledge? How and where would you apply this knowledge to make a decision or change a situation?

4. Choose two obstacles or barriers standing in the way of achieving what you have been trying to do. What step could you take to break the barrier? Do you need to learn something, speak to someone, or change your attitude?

5. When did you last succeed in doing something that you consider "big"? What is the next big thing you would like to accomplish? When and how would you start?

CHAPTER 5

ESTABLISH YOURSELF IN YOUR LIFE'S WORK

There is no passion to be found playing small – in settling for a life that is less than the one you are capable of living.

~ Nelson Mandela ~

I've missed more than 9,000 shots in my career. I've lost almost 300 games. 26 times, I've been trusted to take the game winning shot and missed. I've failed over and over and over again in my life. And that is why I succeed.

~ Michael Jordan ~

When I was thinking about this chapter, the story of the former governor of California flashed through my mind. That man is proof that the world must make room for anyone with the desire and determination to establish themselves in what they have discovered is their exact purpose and calling in life. Arnold Schwarzenegger is not without flaws, but we certainly have a lot to learn from the life of this remarkable personality. Born in 1947, he had a humble start as a child growing up in the strict and harsh post–World War II Austrian society. Interestingly, despite his parents' wishes for him to become a police officer or go to trade school, he formed his own plan for life at the age of fourteen.[1]

Schwarzenegger began his career journey as a bodybuilder, an unpopular sport at that time. Although he did a stint in the

Austrian Army as a tank driver at the age of eighteen—an experience that appealed to the part of him moved by a show of strength—he could not allow anything to dissuade him from his aspiration. He pursued bodybuilding passionately and traveled to London in 1966 to throw his hat in the ring for the Mr. Universe competition. He lost to the American, Chester Yorton, who won because he had better muscle definition in his legs. Schwarzenegger did not give up but agreed to be coached by one of the competition's judges, Charles Bennet, who gave him one of the best opportunities: one-to-one attention and guidance to develop himself.

Through Bennet, Schwarzenegger encountered one of the notable heroes of the Mr. Universe competition, Reg Park, who had won the competition three times with a historic record as only the second person to bench press five hundred pounds. Park became Schwarzenegger's mentor and trainer. Their friendship helped the former governor improve significantly in his time in England. Schwarzenegger went on to win the Mr. Universe competition in 1967 at the age of twenty, becoming the youngest person to win the competition. In fact, he won three more times. He also won the Mr. Olympia title six years in a row, from 1970 to 1975, after which he retired.[2] Then he returned to reclaim the Mr. Olympia title again in 1980. That was just the beginning, as Schwarzenegger always had his eyes on his goals. He wanted to become the greatest actor in the world. He saw his Mr. Universe victory as his ticket to the land of opportunity, America, where he would become a star and get rich. He moved to America, broke into the movie industry, established himself, and eventually became the biggest movie star in the world in the 1990s.

One thing peculiar to those who achieve tremendous success is that they establish themselves in the one thing they have chosen as their pathway in life. Very few humans can be a master of multiple unrelated fields simultaneously. Most renowned people become notable in one endeavor at a time. If I mention the name Michael Jackson, you would think of the King of Pop. What about Albert Einstein, the physicist? And Denzel Washington, the actor? John C. Maxwell, the leadership expert? Ben Carson, the neurosurgeon? Martin Luther King Jr., the civil rights leader? Chimamanda Adichie, the novelist? Steve Harvey, the TV comedian? Babe Ruth, the baseball star? This list goes on. The point is that we associate most successful people with something in particular, the one area that they chose to establish themselves in.

A Jack-of-all-trades is a master of none. Those who jump from occupation to occupation, from career to career, from business to business, from employer to employer, or from trade to trade will find it difficult to be successful in any one thing in particular. Once you have discovered an area where you have a gift, talent, or ability and that you desire to pursue with passion, the only other job you have is to start it and stay with it until you are successful. The beginning of every career journey is usually challenging. As I discussed earlier, there is always a price to pay for

> *There is always a price to pay for the prize. Those who stay, who wait, who push, who keep at it and work it out eventually become established in it.*

the prize. Those who stay, who wait, who push, who keep at it and work it out eventually become established in it. "Rome was not built in a day" as the old saying goes. As part of your plan for success and achievements in life, you must be willing to establish yourself in the area of your life's pursuit. Of course, you can't do anything without a plan, so use these essential categories as a framework.

Define a Clear Direction for Your Life

First determining your destination cannot be overemphasized. Your destination in life should determine the direction of your life. You cannot establish yourself in anything until you have chosen a path you can definitely follow. This concept is straightforward. For example, if you dream of becoming a successful and notable attorney at law and you have chosen to pursue that dream, then your plans and actions will need to align with that choice. You will plan to go to school to take courses that will lead you into law school. If you are asked why you chose certain courses over others, you will explain that those are the courses required for admission into law school. In other words, your career direction becomes clear because you have determined your destination.

I have made an observation. When we face a crossroads in life and do not know which way to go, it is likely we have not defined a destination for ourselves, or we are lacking some necessary knowledge. An example would help here. A high school student who has determined that they will become a professional engineer in the future will not need to think twice when given a choice between taking a physics class or a religion class. If this student has not yet dreamed of a future destination, therefore has no definite direction or ambition yet, they would see the same situation as a dilemma, not knowing what to choose.

Just think about your own choices. Anytime you find yourself at a crossroads, ask yourself if you really know where you were going in the first place. Do you find yourself torn between choices regularly? You may need to check to see if you have defined a definite destination. We make choices daily, and our choices must align with our dreams, what we envision for our lives. Choices become easier when we have a definite destination for life. This applies to every area of life: who to marry, what occupation, where to live, what to learn, what to buy, where to go, et cetera.

The danger of living without knowing the exact destination of your life is that every direction will seem right to you. Without an exact destination in mind, we cannot live life deliberately. We end up floating through a mediocre life without meaning. It is true that there are lots of unknowns and uncertainties in life. How much easier would it be to deal with the unknowns and uncertainties as they occur if you had a concrete

> *The danger of living without knowing the exact destination of your life is that every direction will seem right to you.*

destination? The only thing that should determine the direction of your life is your destination. Most roads are risky. But with a definite destination, those unknowns and uncertainties and risks seem less scary. So whatever road you travel, make sure it leads you to your destination.

Here is the key point. You cannot establish yourself in what you have not defined. You need a definite, specific, and clear direction first. To become an achiever, a person of significance, and a successful individual, you need to have a definite "whereto" for life. The whereto of your life, which you have determined based on your purpose in life, will guide you through the decisions and choices of life. You will find it easier to make choices when you know where you are definitely going.

Choose a Definite Life's Work

Your life's work is that which is the most consistently important activity to you and to which you have decided to dedicate the most substantial part of your effort in life without being under any obligation except that which you have placed on yourself. In other words, your life's work is your main work, the principal activities you base your life's achievements on. Life's work is not the same thing as a job. A job is what you do whether regularly or occasionally for pay. A job is a duty fulfilled for a remuneration. Therefore, most people with jobs are obligated to do what they are doing. That creates an unfortunate situation: many people spend their lives in jobs without ever discovering their life's work. Yes, you can spend your lifetime in jobs that have little or nothing to do with your life's work. Most people do.

One major key to success and fulfillment in life is to find and then choose to embrace our life's work. Let us break this down a little bit. Your life's work should be based on your life's purpose, which we discussed earlier. We noted that the purpose of a thing has a direct relationship with the potential of the thing, and that you can find your life's purpose by discovering your own potential and asking yourself how it can make the world better. Remember, a thing's purpose is to work for something else. In the introduction, I did mention that the pursuit of personal leadership consists not only of your latent gifts, talents, and abilities but also activating your achievements in life using those gifts and abilities. Part of the pursuit of personal leadership is working inside our own life's work, not outside our life's work. Your life's work should be that which allows you to continuously develop and grow in the areas of your gifts, talents, and abilities and consequently leads to your achievements and success.

This is how it works. You discover what you have potential to do; everyone is born with potential. Align your passions with your potential. Your passion is the motivating desire to achieve remarkable things in life using your potential and whatever abilities or resources are available to you. It is the fuel for your achievements in life. A passionate person is difficult to stop. Becoming passionate will challenge you to seek ways to become successful, thereby helping you get creative with your potential, gifts, talents, and abilities.

Passion fires creative thinking. What can you do with what you have? The process of creative thinking will help you develop your own ideas. That leads to envisioning your future based on those ideas. So, your vision *is* your destination, which determines the direction you will take in life. Your life's work is then a collection of activities you must consistently do to become successful in the direction you have chosen as you travel toward your destination. The figure on page ninety-four is an illustration of this process in seven distinct steps. Of course, this is not a rule but a general guideline on how we may find our life's work.

Horst Schulze found his direction for life early, at the age of eleven, and subsequently got into his life's work at the age of fourteen. Born in Germany in 1939, Schulze knew he wanted to work in the hotel business by the time he was eleven.[3] His parents initially hoped he would pursue a technical career such as a technician, architect, or engineer. However, as he said, "I begged my parents to be in the hotel business ... on my knees." After three years of begging them, his parents found him a job as a busboy in a hotel about a hundred kilometers away from their village. It was Schulze's first time in a hotel, ever. He was trained by the headwaiter, who became a model of excellence to him even as a Schulze toiled as a kitchen helper.

Schulze attended hospitality training classes on Wednesdays while working on other days. After about a year and half in the trade school, at sixteen, he was asked to write an essay about his thoughts on the hotel service business. This assignment and his training by the headwaiter inspired him to start defining his role

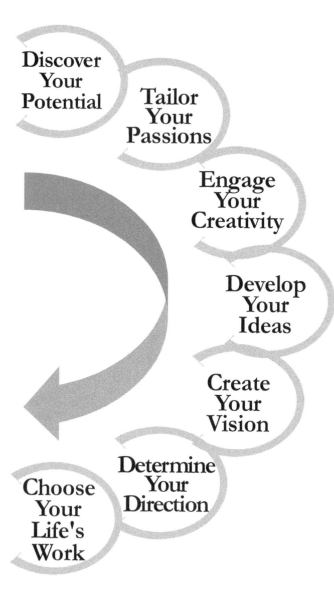

Seven-step process describing how you may find
your life's work

in hospitality as providing excellence in service delivery and caring for the people he served. Then at nineteen, Schulze visited America for the first time while working as a waiter on the Holland America cruise ship. Throughout his early twenties, he worked in various jobs in the hospitality industry to gain experience for his life's work. Among the finest hotels he worked for are the Savoy in London and the Bellevue Palace in Switzerland.

Eventually, in pursuit of his life's work, Schulze took a one-way cruise to America at the age of twenty-five and with only forty dollars in hand. He started out working in a new hotel in Texas but quit after a few days to work at a French restaurant in San Francisco. He wished to be promoted to room-service waiter but could not get this promotion. So, he decided to invest his late twenties and early thirties in studying more by enrolling in courses in hotel management at Cornell University. For seven consecutive summers, he used his vacation days to complete his classes. He grew in his career significantly during those years.

Schulze turned down an offer as general manager at Hyatt Hotels Corporation in his mid-thirties, citing his need for one year of work experience in rooms management. But in his late thirties, he accepted an offer as general manager of the most challenging Hyatt in Pittsburg: the former Howard Johnson Hotel. There he met his wife, Sheri. In his mid-forties in 1983, Schulze became a founding member of The Ritz-Carton Hotel Company, LLC, a business that, in 2021, had 104 hotels with 28,560 rooms in operation and 40 hotels with 7,636 rooms in the pipeline.[4,5]

Like Horst Schulze and Arnold Schwarzenegger, do you know your life's work? Although Schulze found his life's work at an early age, the exact age that we unearth our life's work does not matter as much as the fact that we find it. Many successful, celebrated, and notable people now and historically did not start in their life's work until much later in life. This is because everyone's life journey is different. Age is not an excuse for giving up on the pursuit of personal leadership. Some people find and begin their life's work early while others do not start until much later, just as the historic Moses led the people of Israel, which was his life's work, at the age of eighty. In fact, I know of an African highlife musician and guitarist known as Fatai Rolling Dollar, who was popular in the 1950s and 1960s but disappeared from the music scene for close to three decades, living in penury. Fortunately, he did not give up during those years but kept his musical talent alive while he performed occasionally whenever the opportunity was available. Rolling Dollar eventually made a comeback in 2004 with his song, *"Won Kere si Number Wa,"* which became an instant hit. He died in 2013 at the age of eighty-five, so he made his comeback and achieved success at seventy-four. Age is not an excuse. Choose a definite life's work and pursue it.

Increase Your Personal Value

Most people make one common mistake: we exchange our time for money. People think that to get money, you need to spend your time doing a job and receiving pay. That thinking makes people take on additional hours of work, so they can earn more money. It is the reason many people work multiple jobs, exchanging the scarcest resource on our planet, time, for making ends meet. Some even think they can become rich by working harder and working longer hours or working multiple jobs.

Let me explain why exchanging more time for more money is a big mistake. Two people may work in the same field but receive different amounts of pay at the end of the same amount of time. Why would one person earn more than the other person? If you were working in a grocery store as the store manager, why would your employer pay you more than he would the cashier? The answer is not because you spend more time doing your job than the cashier. It is because your job has a wider scope of responsibility and carries more risk compared to that of the cashier. Apart from the fact that you take responsibility for the cashier's work, you are also responsible for other aspects of the store's functions, including inventory, human resources, pricing, supplier relationships, customer experience, and facilities management. The company could easily replace the cashier but not as easily replace you because of your special knowledge and skill in managing a grocery business. In other words, the organization attaches more economic value to your work and pays you accordingly.

So what do we actually pay for? When you hire a plumber to work on your sinks and drains, what are you paying for? Why do you pay your lawyer so much, but you pay a general laborer so much less? It turns out we tend to pay for "value." You are not paid according to the amount of time you spend on your job or the effort you expend. You are paid according to the value you deliver in your job. You cannot increase the amount of time you have because time is a fixed resource, but you can increase the value you bring to whatever you do. Time does not add value to us. We add value to our time. When we become more valuable, our time becomes a precious commodity.

You cannot increase the amount of time you have because time is a fixed resource, but you can increase the value you bring to whatever you do. Time does not add value to us. We add value to our time. When we become more valuable, our time becomes a precious commodity.

Everyone can become more valuable. *You* can become more valuable. If you are not satisfied with your current earnings, ask yourself if you can become more valuable. If your effort is valued at fifteen dollars per hour in your job, can you increase that to thirty dollars per hour? What about two hundred dollars per hour? What could you do to make that happen? Is there a new knowledge or skill you need to acquire? Do you need to learn a new trade? How can you improve yourself and thereby increase how much someone is willing to pay for your effort? How much more valuable can you become? I once heard of a consultant who charged five thousand dollars per hour for his services, yes, five thousand dollars per hour. That is how valuable his time was.

Here is the truth. The more valuable you are, the more wealth, achievements, and successes you can attract to yourself. Unless one inherits a pot of gold, the only thing we can exchange for fortune in life is value. Just look at an apple tree. What attracts you to the tree is the fruit: the value that you derive from the tree. If the tree bears no fruit during the fruit season, you may not place any value on the tree. In fact, what makes the tree valuable is the fruit, without which the tree may lose its value.

> *Unless one inherits a pot of gold, the only thing we can exchange for fortune in life is value.*

Have you considered that you are just like the apple tree? When you pursue personal leadership and work toward your destination, people are attracted to you because you bear fruit; you are valuable, and they call you successful. When you plant yourself where you get water and fertilizer, equipping yourself with what you need to get ahead in life, you improve your ability to bear fruit. People are then attracted to you because you are bountiful; you yield value. If you have what people need, they will find you and pay you for it.

The key message here is that it is your responsibility to invest in your personal growth and development. As part of your effort to establish yourself in your life's work, you must continue to improve your self-worth by adding value to yourself, getting all the skills, training, information, education, and self-improvement you need to become more valuable. Your time will be worth increasingly more as you increase your self-worth and as you use your knowledge and experience to effect change in the world. As discussed earlier, wisdom is the application of knowledge. Becoming more valuable means becoming wiser in your approach to life and in your pursuit of personal leadership.

Develop Expertise

Developing expertise is about getting good at what you do. Your aim in life should be to become the best in whatever you have chosen as your life's work. In your life's work, you are competing with yourself. The race is unending, and you must keep getting better as time passes. The goal is for you to become established; gain well-rounded knowledge, skill, and experience in your life's work; and become resourcefully authoritative in your work. If you master your art well enough, you will be called skillful, and those who need what you produce will gravitate to you.

If you are a computer programmer, learn the skills to code so well people call you a wizard. If you are a musician, let them call you a virtuoso. If you are an architect, let the world call you a crackerjack. Become the best painter in town, the best electrician, the best waiter, the best athlete, the best optician, the best dentist, the best schoolteacher, the best janitor, the best priest—just be the best of whosoever you are. Become exceptionally good at what you do and continuously improve your expertise such that only a few people, if any at all, can match you. It is in becoming your very best that you become the first. It is in the pursuit of personal leadership *in the area of your expertise* that you will reach the pinnacle of achievement and become successful in life.

Let me tell you a secret. There is actually no talent anywhere, except the one that is developed. All talents and skills are latent, only potential, until they are developed. How developed your talent becomes determines how exceptional you become. The more exceptional you become, the more successful you become in life. It is by developing expertise that we create a niche for ourselves, thereby increasing our value. People stand out in their own niche.

> *There is actually no talent anywhere, except the one that is developed. All talents and skills are latent, only potential, until they are developed.*

A sick person would prefer to be treated by the best doctor. I prefer the best teacher be assigned as my child's teacher. If all mechanics in town charge similar amounts, I would send my car to be fixed by the best. In fact, I would pay a premium to get my car fixed by the best mechanic. People that become the best and offer the best get all the attention they need to become successful, whereas mediocrity, lack of expertise, and unskillfulness relegate one to the realm of ordinariness or even perpetual failure. In your pursuit, determine to become excellent at what you do. Develop your expertise. Do whatever it takes: classes, courses, webinars, podcasts, volunteering, taking chances, et cetera.

Stay Focused

Distraction is one enemy of personal achievements. Many people lose track of their destination because of distraction. If you are playing a game of table tennis, or ping pong, one thing you must master is focus. You do not know what your opponent will do. You must stay focused on the ball as it moves back and forth on the table. Otherwise, you will miss and lose the game. It is the same with whatsoever remarkable thing we are trying to achieve in life. We must keep our focus on the ball. We must ensure we avoid distractions.

A high school senior, a peer of mine and one of the most brilliant students in his set, was accepted into university to study agriculture. He soon realized that he did not want a career in agriculture but would rather study electrical engineering. While in the first year of the agriculture program, he processed another admission into the same university for electrical engineering. So, though he had completed year-one courses while in the agriculture program, he needed to start all over again in the electrical engineering program as the course content did not exactly match the agriculture requirements. Nevertheless, he finished his first year in the agriculture program with flying colors as he had always been a notably brilliant student.

On beginning the electrical engineering program the following year, the year-one courses were easy for him. He had mastered year-one courses the previous year and just needed to study a few more things to perform well in the new year-one courses. He had so much time on his hands that he decided to fill it with something else. Chess became that something else. He got so good at it that after a while, playing chess became an obsession. Without any real intention to become a professional chess player, he stopped attending classes and devoted more time to challenging his friends to chess every day because it was popular on campus then.

This fellow completed year one in the electrical engineering program, this time again with the best grades anyone could wish to have; he was a brilliant student after all. He did not need to study hard or attend all his classes; his residual knowledge from his previous year one was an advantage. He devoted more time to playing chess and having a good time with friends. Then the second year began, but he had formed a habit of not attending classes and just playing chess all day. His grades began to drop. By the time he completed the second year, his cumulative grade-point average was at rock bottom. Therefore, he needed to leave the university in his third year, and he dropped out of the program. While there was nothing wrong with playing chess, he allowed it to become a distraction, and it cost him his opportunity to become an electrical engineer. He still managed to study in a related field at another university later, but he had lost many years, graduating five years after his counterparts.

While working to classify people according to their propensity to focus, I realized that there are four categories. The first category includes those who *lack* focus. These people do not generally focus on anything. Those who lack focus usually have no drive for personal achievement as long as they have enough to get through life. They just watch everything as it all happens around them. Their approach to life is simplistic and does not demand they contribute anything significant to their personal or professional development.

The second category includes those who have *lost* focus. These people had a specific direction for life but lost focus on their destination before they could arrive. Many people start out well in life, with ambitions and aspirations and goals that could get them where they needed to go. Unfortunately, they did not realize their goals because they got distracted, lost interest, or encountered unforeseen circumstances. Some just settle for less after becoming distracted because it ends up costing more to continue to strive to reach their goals. Others lose heart after experiencing unforeseen circumstances. They lose the desire to focus and would rather just let go and slide through life in mediocrity.

The third category includes those with a "dilly-dally" focus. Those with a dilly-dally focus do not focus on anything in particular. Their focus changes depending on the opportunity. They are moved only by what is "selling" out there. Yesterday they were bankers, today they are engineers, and tomorrow they may be real-estate agents. They are the "Jack-of-all-trades, master of none." Those with a dilly-dally focus end up achieving much less than expected and, in most cases, do not have much to show for several years of laboring.

The fourth category includes those who have intense, continuous focus. These people center their interests, passion, and effort on their life's work and do not waver from achieving what they have determined to pursue. They are tenacious, diligent, unrelenting, hardworking, and dedicated and are willing to pay the price for achieving

> *Just like an eagle narrows its long-range vision to focus on its prey, so should anyone aspiring to achieve success and greatness in life focus on whatsoever they have determined to accomplish.*

something worthwhile. Everyone must learn to maintain focus. Without focus, it is hard for anyone to establish themselves in their life's work. The temptation of distraction will always be there. However, just like an eagle narrows its long-range vision to focus on its prey, so should anyone aspiring to achieve success and greatness in life focus on whatsoever they have determined to accomplish.

Multiply Your Success

Most successful individuals and organizations dominate their fields of endeavor, exercising some form of command, influence, or control over the affairs. Those who are successful continue to multiply their success until they establish dominance in their areas. This is an important point.

Let us look at it purely from a business point of view. If you were a manufacturer, your ability to record tremendous success would depend on how many products you can both produce and sell in any given period. Meanwhile, selling many of your products is only one level of success. Success begins with your ability to make the product in the first place. It might have taken you many years of continuous effort to make your product. From that first level of making a marketable product, you need to proceed to being able to generate demand, then you need to fulfill that demand. You may need to work on quality, marketing, branding, and market differentiators that can help boost the success of your product. If you were making and selling from a single location, you may want to expand to multiple locations and capture new markets. As your business grows, you begin to establish some form of dominance.

Look at it this way. What if MacDonald's, Burger King, or KFC had maintained just one physical location from their inception until now, just serving their loyal customers but making no effort to expand and dominate the industry? Did you know Amazon was not the only online retail store when it was founded? What about the stories of Apple, Microsoft, General Electric, Tesla, and other successful businesses? Why do companies engage in mergers and acquisitions and horizontal and vertical integration? Is the pattern not that of an attempt to exercise control, to influence or command their respective industries? That is dominating in your life's work.

Why am I citing these examples? It is the same for organizations as it is for individuals. In your life's work, seek to establish yourself to the extent that you exercise some form of command, influence, or control in your field. Create the best quality of whatsoever you produce. Differentiate yourself in your marketplace or in your field of endeavor. Capture a large segment of your marketplace. Replicate the fruit of your life and make it available for the whole world to access. Reproduce yourself everywhere and in every way. Hone your skill and increase your value. Convince the whole world that you have the best to offer and let them prefer whatsoever you have. Establish yourself in your life's work.

CHAPTER 5 DISCOVERY QUESTIONS

1. Do you know your life's work yet? If yes, write it down below. If no, think through the seven steps discussed in this chapter and begin a journey to choosing your life's work.

2. Thinking about the job or career you are currently pursuing, would that lead you to your life's work? Are there systematic adjustments you can make to get closer to your life's work?

3. On a scale of 1 to 5, 1 being the lowest and 5 being the highest, how proficient are you in your area of expertise, trade, or vocation? If you were low on the scale, identify what you need to develop to improve your expertise.

4. Write down one thing that distracts you the most in your pursuit of personal leadership. How would you address the distraction? If it is a necessary distraction, what alternative actions can you take?

5. What would you need to do to establish some dominance in your profession, career, vocation, trade, or work? Read the section, "Multiply Your Success" again for help.

CHAPTER 6

EXPLOIT YOUR CREATIVE-THINKING ABILITY

The world always seems brighter when you've just made some-thing that wasn't there before.

~ Neil Gaiman ~

If you keep colouring within the boxes and writing on the lines, you may never be able to do something remarkable. Break your spirit free to explore.

~ Bernard Kelvin Clive ~

In principle, your ability to think creatively is one of the most important contributors to your chances of succeeding in anything.

What it takes to stand out from the crowd and do something extraordinary or outstanding is not as daunting as we assume. Many of us engage our minds in average-value thoughts because, truly, only a handful of human beings have a genius in anything. But we do not necessarily need the ingenuity of Albert Einstein or the artistry of Beethoven to get ahead in life. I have observed that most people remain in mediocrity because they assume creativity is exclusive to a certain class of individuals. Yet if you deviate even slightly from that average thinking, you can earn the future you have always dreamed of.

Let me give you an example. I was in a meeting with some stakeholders of various organizations in winter 2021. The meeting was winding down when the moderator asked the attendees to share new things going on in their lives or careers. I decided to use that opportunity to tell the team about my book, *Be a Change Agent: Leadership in a Time of Exponential Change*. Though everyone was positive and encouraging, one attendee made a comment that stunned me. This person congratulated me and then said, "I cannot even think of writing a book." Note that this person did not say, "I don't have the potential to write a book," but, "I cannot even think …"

Writing a book requires that we *think* about it first. Writing a good book requires creative thinking, and you need to step out of everyday, average thinking to do it. Creativity is using our imagination to bring about something new, original, or unusual. It all starts with creative thinking. And note the word "unusual." That implies there are many regular or usual things out there. The world is full of similar things simply replicated by the majority. We are all so used to our current environment, to normal, to usual, to ordinary, that we need to step out of our current thinking to become creative. Creative thinking is an ability we must deliberately cultivate and intentionally exploit. Every one of us has the potential to develop our creative-thinking ability.

Whenever the word, "creativity," is used, we tend to think only about forming or making something entirely new or novel, something that has not been done before. Or we think about those fabulously talented artistic folk who paint or whittle or blow glass. While that is partly true, we need to understand that creative thinking can also result in the discovery, innovation, or creation of something new out of what is available. A discovery may be something entirely new—a product, process, or idea—that has not been used or found before, such as when Alexander Graham

Bell invented the telephone. Or creative thinking could unearth a new way of doing something or a way to make something easier. Innovation is often confused with invention, but it actually refers to adapting something that already exists. Innovation takes an existing idea, concept, or invention to a completely new level.

Let's look at an example. The LED light bulb was an invention, but we can regard its use in car headlights as an innovation. The electric motor was an invention, but its use in powering machinery required adaptation, in other words, innovation. Many music styles—jazz, hip-hop, rock, classical, afro-beat—were invented but have been adapted by innovative musicians over the years. Artistry inventions such as stained glass, sculpture, oil painting, and pottery are still being innovatively used today. The reality is that most of us may not necessarily discover something brand new. Some will harness their creative-thinking ability to break new ground and make discoveries while others will use innovative thinking to improvise and bring about other ideas, concepts, products, processes, and solutions based on what already exists. Both discovering and innovating are results of creative thinking.

Here are the nine characteristics of creative thinking:

1. Creative thinking requires imagination and hard mental work. If it was easy to come by, someone would have found it a long time ago.
2. Creative thinking involves questioning norms and attempting to answer questions.
3. Creative thinking usually deviates from, builds upon, or defies conventional or rational thinking.
4. Creative thinking makes the thinker see things the way they could be rather than the way they are.

5. Creative thinking helps connect the dots, bringing unconnected things together to define something meaningful.

6. Creative thinking is open to ambiguity, uncertainties, and alternatives without trying to align with a perfect picture of anything.

7. Creative thinking is aware of facts, principles, and reality and seeks ways to leverage existing ideas in an unusual way.

8. Creative thinking produces new or unusual ideas, and sometimes manifold ideas, which have the potential to lead to discoveries, inventions, and innovations.

9. Creative thinking leads to more creative thinking.

Develop Your Capacity for Creative Thinking

Developing capacity for creative thinking is hard work. Training the mind to come up with creative ideas requires deliberate and specific actions. To develop the capacity for creative thinking, both you and I need to consistently take the following actions:

1. Be inquisitive and observant

A curious mind desires to know as much as possible about things, events, circumstances, and its environment. The more inquisitive you are, the more likely you are to see, perceive, or discover what is not obvious to others. A person eager to know much about something is in a position to uncover facts and discover new things. Curiosity coupled with careful observation is the recipe for creativity. In fact, most

The more inquisitive you are, the more likely you are to see, perceive, or discover what is not obvious to others.

known discoveries in various fields were made by observation powered by inquisitiveness. Let us look at a few examples from science.

The American scientist and inventor, Percy Spencer, conducted laboratory experiments on high-powered vacuum tubes, or magnetrons, inside radar. On one fateful day in 1945 while Spencer was working near magnetrons that produced radiation in the microwave range, he noticed that a peanut butter candy bar in his pocket got warm and melted. He decided to experiment with popcorn, and it started to pop. Then, he tried other food items. The rest is history. Spencer invented the microwave oven, which his employer, Raytheon, patented and developed.[1] The microwave oven became a necessary household appliance whose sales surpassed those of gas ranges by 1975. In 1999, Spencer became immortalized for his invention of the microwave oven and was inducted into the National Inventors Hall of Fame, classing him among other inventors like Thomas Edison and the Wright brothers. Spencer had observed and inquired and discovered something new.

Before the 1940s, there was no effective treatment for infectious diseases such as pneumonia, gonorrhea, and rheumatic fever. In those days, people suffered from blood poisoning contracted from cuts and scratches because doctors could not do much but wait and hope patients recovered. Many patients did not recover; they died of their infections. Though antibiotics produced from bacteria and fungi were historically known to be capable of killing some microbial species—even the ancient Egyptians applied a poultice of moldy bread to infected wounds[2]—scientists of the day were not observant or inquisitive enough, so antibiotics used in therapeutic medicine was not even discovered in the modern world until 1928 and not standard practice until the 1940s.

Early in his medical career, Professor of Bacteriology Sir Alexander Fleming, made one of the most important discoveries in the history of therapeutic medicine. He worked extensively on the study of the natural bacterial action of the blood and antiseptics.[3] On September 3, 1928, Fleming was sorting through petri dishes of bacteria colonies that cause boils, sore throats, and abscesses when he observed something unusual. One of the petri dishes contained dotted colonies, though those colonies were absent in an area around where a blob of mold was growing. Fleming found that the "mold juice" was surrounded by a clear zone, which looked as if the mold was secreting an inhibiting substance preventing bacterial growth. Further experiments proved the mold juice could kill a wide range of harmful bacteria.

Fleming tasked his assistants, Stuart Craddock and Frederick Ridley, with isolating the inhibiting substance from the mold juice. This pure substance was penicillin, the very substance that heralded the era of developing antibiotics for therapeutic medicine. After several years of research by Oxford University and many British and American companies, penicillin made clinical trials in the early 1940s in the United States, and again, the rest is history. Sir Alexander Fleming received the 1945 Nobel Prize in Physiology or Medicine by being observant and inquisitive and discovering something new.

One may easily misconstrue the observations that led to the invention of the microwave oven and the discovery of penicillin as experimental accidents. That notion would undermine the creative-thinking process necessary for arriving at those profound observations. No one *stumbles* upon the discovery of penicillin or the invention of the microwave oven. People who deploy their curious minds in creatively thinking about possibilities after making observations are those who make discoveries and inventions.

Becoming inquisitive and observant does not apply only to science. For example, those who continue to be inquisitive as they too master their work in the arts and humanities are those who see new possibilities. For example, many talented musicians are excellent songwriters, vocalists, or instrumentalists who become inspired as they diligently master their art, and they create new music and new music styles. By paying attention to minute details in our daily work and meditating on it, we place ourselves in a better position to be creative.

2. Create time and space for creative thinking

Tapping into the information bank within one's subconscious mind requires focused thinking. To have focused thinking, one must devote time to thinking. Having a dedicated thinking time may sound like a strange idea, but it is critical for achieving results.

Similarly, the boisterousness of our daily environment, with the hustle and bustle of city lives, noisy workplaces, mobile distractions, and always having people around us may require that we have a designated place or space for creative thinking. Both time and space help us to create an environment for focused thinking.

When it comes to creating time and space for creative thinking, everyone has different needs. Some examples of environments, activities, or situations that foster focused creative thinking may include, but are not limited to, the following:

- during a personal retreat somewhere exclusive, away from home and work
- behind the closed doors of an office or a focus room used by only one person at a time

- during a walk in a park or an environment with natural views such as beaches or forests
- when lying quietly in bed at night or just waking up in the morning
- while reading in a quiet part of a library or at home when it is quiet
- in any quiet place designated as a thinking place

During the process of deliberate creative thinking, the conscious mind focuses its attention on a particular subject and draws from the information bank within the subconscious mind. Using a personal computer as an example, the subconscious mind works like a hard disk while the conscious mind works like random access memory, or RAM. The conscious mind, RAM, handles information currently in use by the brain but calls up information already stored in the subconscious mind, the hard disk, during the thinking process. This act, also sometimes referred to as meditation, is the means by which humans can tap into their personal creativity. It requires focus and the dedication of a specific time and place to accomplish.

The human subconscious mind is full of treasures that can be converted into creative thoughts and subsequently workable ideas. You can access the treasures in the conscious mind during meditation by engaging, deliberately, your thinking capacity.

Meditation simply means thinking or pondering. It is not supposed to be a mystical, occultist practice. Meditation is the means through which we mine our creative thinking. During mediation, we focus our thoughts on something in particular. For example, the content of this book is mostly a product of my personal meditation. I spent a significant amount of time thinking through what to say and how to say it. I focused my thoughts on one section at a time, and I pondered over my experiences and life lessons to draw out the most important points to share with you. If you are trying to make a significant decision, design a new product, start a new career, go to college, build a business, or anything else that may feel difficult, meditation can help you come up with creative ideas. You may just need to think things through.

In addition, meditation does not have to be a formal practice. You can meditate while driving, showering, or waiting in line. You can meditate for a few minutes or a few hours. Remember that mediation is all about focused thinking, which helps you to access and tie together thoughts and ideas you would not have discovered otherwise.

3. Adopt the heart of a child and use your imagination

My son, just before he turned seven, told me his idea. When he becomes an adult, he said, he wants to build a mansion so big it would house everyone in his large family, including his parents and his cousins and their families. The mansion would have a big yard and gardens, spacious bedrooms, large kitchen and dining areas, and more. What surprised me was that he seemed to have figured out exactly what he wanted and how it would look. He explained things in some detail.

His only challenge was that he would not be able to maintain and keep the house all by himself. He would need people to help him every day. He said, "Dad, I don't want to use people as slaves in my mansion." So, I explained that he would not have to use people as slaves because as we've discussed in developing your life's blueprint, he would just need ask for help from others, in other words, hire people for decent wages and treat them with respect. However, I did ask him to include a pad on the property for landing my helicopter. I also let him know that his dream was valid, and he could achieve whatever his mind could conceive.

Children are very imaginative, mostly because they do not know much yet. They are full of hope and empty of fear. Many of the things that we adults know do not limit them. Our biggest issue as adults is that we lose the heart of a child as we grow up. As we acquire experience and face the facts of life, we jettison our creative-thinking ability. We lose our natural ability to be imaginative. In fact, some of the barriers to creativity include expertise and experience. The training, facts, experience, and expertise we gather over time become the constraints of our imagination. Creative thinking requires us to step outside the box to explore not what is already in the box, but what is outside the box. To be creative in our thinking is to adopt the heart of a child, to dream again, to get comfortable with the unusual.

> *Our biggest issue as adults is that we lose the heart of a child as we grow up. As we acquire experience and face the facts of life, we jettison our creative-thinking ability. We lose our natural ability to be imaginative.*

This discussion brings the story of the biblical Joseph to mind. Permit me to interpret his experience this way. In his imagination as a child, he was going to become so great in the social and political landscape of his time that even those supposedly superior to him would accord him the greatest respect. In the words of a child, he said that the sun, the moon, and eleven stars would bow down to him. Joseph was creative in all his life adventures, including his ordeals, and eventually became the administrator of the most civilized society of his time: Egypt. To think creatively is to break free from narrow-mindedness, to widen our horizon, to become imaginative, and to think the seemingly impossible without fear or constraint.

4. Write down your thoughts and ideas

How many times have you struggled to remember that great idea that crossed your mind yesterday, last week, or last year? One of the best ways to remember your thoughts is to write them down, on paper or electronic devices. Shaping your ideas becomes easier if you write them down exactly the way you thought about them. Give yourself an opportunity to revisit your creative thoughts and analyze, add to, improve, update, and expand your thoughts.

This book was initially only a thought in my mind, a thought about how most of us want our lives to count for something though we have yet to figure out how to make it happen. But I did not take my thought for granted. I spent more time thinking about my own and other successful people's experiences and how to capture them to help others grow. In my first hour of engaging my creative thinking on this subject, I wrote down eleven salient points that I eventually further developed and refined to become this entire book.

If you have imagined something great, could you try to represent your imagination in pictures or with descriptions? If you are creatively thinking about building a business, could you write down a few ideas that you can develop into a business plan? If you are creatively thinking about the results of your scientific experiments, could you write down your interpretation of the results? If you are creatively thinking about a new song, could you write down a few lines of the song and the music that goes along with it?

Do not assume you will remember everything. Many thoughts cross our minds daily. Unwritten creative thoughts may eventually get lost amid thousands of other thoughts.

5. Think through and work through ideas

Allow your ideas to multiply and think through alternatives. Realize that there is no one perfect way of doing anything. Don't reject an idea as silly. Write them all down and consider them all. Having only one idea and focusing only on that one idea is not the way to develop creative-thinking capacity. When we conceive an idea, we should let that idea lead us to other ideas, and we should continue to shape those ideas until we arrive at a breakthrough idea. Creative thinkers do not jump to conclusions just because they got one great idea. We continue to shape, improve, and redevelop ideas until they become inventions and innovations. Creative thinking requires flexible thinking.

It is necessary for us to allow sufficient time for ideas to fully form. Your best idea yesterday may look foolish to you today. That is why you must think through your ideas. Once you have written down the results of your creative thinking, wait for a few days or even months. During those days and months, expose yourself to new information, methods, and processes that can help you improve your idea. Then revisit your idea and continue to shape it. In most cases, we need to experiment with our ideas and continue to gather useful information to help us think more creatively about our ideas.

One of the greatest minds in history, who thought through and worked through his ideas, was the famous scientist and inventor Thomas Edison. He was famously known to have invented the incandescent electric light bulb after significant time spent thinking through and working through his idea. He also invented many other products including the cylinder phonograph, carbon microphone, tasimeter, movie camera and viewer, and alkaline storage battery.

6. Make room for collective thinking

During the First World War, spinal injury and gunshot wounds resulted in almost certain death from the infection that followed. These fatalities reduced drastically during the Second World War after the discovery of penicillin, such that the survival rate climbed to 80 to 90 percent. Though a positive outcome, higher survival rates created another challenge: many survivors became quadriplegics. John Counsell, a Canadian officer, was one of those survivors. Counsell was shot through the back and would live the rest of his life with paraplegia. He ended up in a manual wheelchair. He soon realized that quadriplegics needed more than a manual wheelchair and started an advocacy that attracted Canada's commitment to the healthcare support of veterans post-war. This led to a request of the National Research Council of Canada (NRC) to build an entirely new type of wheelchair.[4]

The responsibility of developing a new wheelchair was given to the renowned Canadian inventor, George Klein, who worked as a mechanical engineer and designer at the NRC labs in Ottawa. Klein worked with other professionals to invent the first mass-produced electric wheelchair. He developed the wheel drive, turning systems, and joystick, the same technologies that still feature in today's electric wheelchair. Canadian veterans were the first to be given the electric wheelchair. International efforts to commercialize the electric wheelchair led to the formal transfer of patent-free rights to the US Department of Veterans Affairs to encourage production in the US. The wheelchair eventually became available to both veterans and civilians in large numbers.

One of the most significant parts of Klein's approach to the invention of the electric wheelchair was his collaborative effort, having engaged healthcare workers, doctors, other mechanical and electrical engineers, administrators, and patients in the thinking process that led to the invention. Although we can credit

Klein with inventing the first electric wheelchair, he approached his work from a perspective of "collective thinking." He used his creative-thinking ability but also employed collective creative thinking to bring an invention to life, one that became an integral pillar in providing care for people with physical handicap.

How does your creative idea fit into the whole of society? Do you employ collective thinking with others during your creative thinking? How can you creatively combine your ideas with those of others to make the world a better place? No single individual is an island of creative thoughts. Most inventors and creators work with others and take a collective-thinking approach. Artists and crafts-people have apprentices and peers. Scientists have research assistants and colleagues. Musicians have bands and mentors. Lions have a pride and a social order. In developing your capacity for creative thinking, consider and be open to ideas generated through collaboration and the strength of collective thoughts of similarly great minds.

> *No single individual is an island of creative thoughts. Most inventors and creators work with others and take a collective thinking approach.*

7. Learn to believe

If you do not believe in your own creative thoughts, you cannot expect anyone else to believe in them. Using our creative thoughts to produce something tangible or significant in the world requires confidence and belief in our own thoughts. You have probably heard that "seeing is believing." However, "believing is seeing" is more appropriate when thinking about the future. If your mind can conceive it, you can achieve it. To bring our creative thoughts and imaginings, and the resulting ideas, into reality, we must believe in them. Believing comes before seeing.

Napoleon Bonaparte said, "Impossible is a word to be found only in the dictionary of fools." Never say never. Many things humans once thought to be impossible have been achieved. Here are some quotes from experts who suggested some groundbreaking inventions were impossible:

> "Good enough for our transatlantic friends ... but unworthy of the attention of practical or scientific men." That was from a committee set up by the British Parliament to discuss Thomas Edison's claim that he would invent the incandescent bulb.[5]

> "Flight by machines heavier than air is impractical and insignificant, if not utterly impossible," said Simon Newcomb, physicist and director of the US Naval Observatory in 1902.[6]

> "I think there is a world market for maybe five computers," said Thomas Watson, president of IBM in 1943.[7]

When acting on your imagination, you may meet with opposition, differing expert opinions, or even threats. Civil rights leader, Dr. Martin Luther King Junior, imagined something unheard of in his time. He dreamed of ending racism-driven segregation between the "whites" and the "people of color." He believed in what he imagined, stayed focused, and acted unapologetically on his dream until the end of his life. It became a historic turning point. Nelson Mandela imagined a South Africa free of domination by any one race. He believed in his thoughts, acted on his beliefs, and devoted his life to the fight for freedom. The result was an end to apartheid and the minority rule.

While you should be open to reasoning, scrutiny, and ideas from others, do not allow your creative thoughts to become dead on arrival. What you think about your own thoughts and ideas matters more than what others think about your thoughts and ideas. Believe that your creative thoughts are valid and that your imaginings are authentic.

Become a Steward of Your Creative Thoughts

The human mind can access an infinite number of creative thoughts. There are no limits in the world of imagination. Engaging our minds in creative thinking is like living in a perfect world where everything is possible, where there are no constraints on budgets, time, resources, and ideas. Imagine yourself building your dream mansion. Start with a plan. Create all the drawings in your mind. How many rooms do you have? What does the entrance look like? What types of flooring is there? How many living rooms? Now focus on the master bedroom on the second floor. Do you see the double glass doors leading to the private balcony? Step on the balcony and overlook the private lake and the forest in the background.

Continue imagining until you have completed the entire plan. Then, in your imagination, call the property development company and tell them which private island you would like. Now continue imagining in this manner until you have built the entire mansion on the island of your dreams. The purpose of creating this mental picture is to emphasize the fact that imagination has no limits. Meanwhile, the purpose of creative thinking is to bring positive change, improvement, invention, or innovation to the world. None of that can happen if we limit our imagination or neglect to act on it. Our great intentions, excellent creative thoughts, and wonderful imaginings need action. We must become the stewards of our imagination.

President John F. Kennedy, in his famous Rice Stadium moon speech of September 12, 1962, said, "... this country of the United States was not built by those who waited and rested and wished to look behind them. This country was conquered by those who moved forward ..."[8] Only those who move forward achieve anything of substance. Creative thoughts will become ordinary wishes if no action follows. If Walt Disney had kept Mickey Mouse only in his imagination, the legendary cartoon character would not have become the iconic character he is today.

We must all commit ourselves to acting on our creative thoughts and become the stewards of our imagination. Many

> *Creative thoughts will become ordinary wishes if no action follows.*

people are full of extraordinary thoughts that never materialize into anything of value. Creative thinking is not enough. The outcome of creative thinking is ideas waiting to be exploited and birthed into something unusual. Take action. Steward that imagination toward materialization.

Exchange Your Creativity for Value

What is the worth of your creative thought? Let us look at real estate to illustrate this. A homeowner may argue with the real-estate agent that their house is worth a certain cash value. The city's property assessment department may allocate a fair market value to a property. An independent property appraiser may choose a number and call it the value of a property. However, the true value of any property is the amount someone is willing to pay for it. It does not matter how much you or anyone else thinks your property is worth. The real test of value is how much someone is willing to pay.

Our ideas also have worth. You could exchange one idea for only $100 and another for $1,000,000. And there are even more ideas worth substantially more, such that we can say they are invaluable. The good news is that ideas are not as limited as real estate. There is much less constraint when constructing an idea to make it worth more than when constructing real estate. In reality, the outcome of our creative thinking is invaluable, yet we still need to somehow exchange our creativity for value. Our creative thoughts should bring positive value and tangible results both to others and us. For example, if you are a creative and talented singer, could you create songs and be signed by a record label? Exchanging creativity for value means converting your creative thoughts to something upon which we can place financial or economic value or social benefits.

If you were an exceptional painter like Picasso, how could you exchange your creativity for value? If you were an erudite person with the poetic prowess of Shakespeare, what value could that bring to you and the world around you? What if you are creatively thinking for change in business, science, politics, entertainment, sports, et cetera? The whole world is awaiting the manifestation of your brainchild. We are all waiting for you; we are all waiting to witness and enjoy the fruits of your creative thinking. Your creativity may be the source of financial wealth, opportunities, breakthroughs, recognition, or fame for you. It may be the means of livelihood for a host of others. Or it could change how others think or behave or feel. How would your idea affect the world around you? How would you exchange your creativity for value?

Think Creatively for Positive Change

The outcome of creative thinking can be either positive or negative. Some use creative thinking for crime, swindling, machinations, hateful speeches, and so on. Many atrocities committed by humanity have been products of carefully thought-through processes.

My challenge to you is to become a creative thinker for positive change. How would you differentiate between what is positive or negative during creative thinking? Are there principles we may adopt to help us pursue positive creative thinking and dismiss negative creative thinking? I suggest you align your thoughts with the following seven positive-thinking patterns.[9]

1. creatively thinking about what is based on truth as opposed to falsehood and misrepresentation of truth
2. creatively thinking about things that attract honor and dignity for humanity
3. aligning our creative thoughts with things that seek the greater good for all
4. considering ethics, health, well-being, and benefits for others
5. asking if our creative thoughts will bring peace, happiness, and goodwill to us and others
6. considering if the outcome of our creative thoughts will deserve respect
7. attaining excellence in service to humanity

CHAPTER 6 DISCOVERY QUESTIONS

1. Going back to the beginning of this chapter, take some time to reflect on the nine characteristics of creative thinking. Do you think you are a creative thinker? How could you become your best version of a creative thinker?

2. Based on the section on how to develop your capacity for creative thinking, which two of the seven action areas do you need to work on? Which two are your areas of strength?

3. Is there anything you had thought impossible before reading this chapter? Do you really believe you can achieve anything you have set your mind to?

4. Write down one idea of yours that you know can bring significant financial gain to you and others. How could you start implementing the idea?

5. Could you describe your mental picture of your future? If you do not yet have one, I suggest you take some time, follow the action steps in this book, and create one. Then write down your thoughts and develop an action plan.

CHAPTER 7

EXPLORE THE WORLD OF POSSIBILITIES

Success is where preparation and opportunity meet.

~ Bobby Unser ~

You must decide if you are going to rob the world or bless it with the rich, valuable, potent, untapped resources locked away within you.

~ Myles Munroe ~

Where does luck come from? You have probably met or heard of many fortunate people, people who grabbed hold of the best that life can afford. Does it seem to you like there was something accidental about their fortunes? Is there really something like luck in success? Well, we know there is such a thing as time and chance, where a person meets with an opportunity at a particular time. However, we also know that time and chance would mean absolutely nothing to someone who has not prepared for the opportunity at hand. One of the most unfortunate things that can happen to anyone is to be presented with an opportunity but have no wherewithal to take advantage of it due to lack of skills, education, or preparation.

Here is another observation. Not every great musician records hit songs. Not all great athletes make the Olympics. Not all great soccer players make English soccer clubs and play in the Premier League. There are many great books written by great writers but are not discovered. In fact, in a whole century, only about a hundred of the best writers have won the Nobel Prize for literature. This is exactly where time and chance come in. That is why our skills, plans, actions, effort, creativity, and preparation must meet with opportunities. The greatest achievers, those who become successful and fulfilled, are those whose preparations met with opportunities. It does seem these successful people did the right thing at the right time in the right place.

One of the most unfortunate things that can happen to anyone is to be presented with an opportunity but have no wherewithal to take advantage of it due to lack of skills, education, or preparation.

However, no one just sits and waits for opportunities. Like the legendary African musician, Beautiful Nubia said, "True freedom does not come to those who sit and pray." We have a role to play to improve our chances of success. Opportunities are everywhere but we need to make ourselves visible to them. The subject of this chapter is crucial. It is not enough to be exceptional at what we do. We need to open ourselves up to the world of opportunities and possibilities. We need to be willing to do what is needed to allow the best of our preparations for achievement to be fitted with the best of opportunities.

A notable mathematician lived around the turn of the nineteenth century. He was the pioneer of many discoveries in what mathematicians call, "partition functions," in the theory of numbers. Srinivasa Ramanujan was born in 1887 in Erode, India, but lived only thirty-two years. He attained a significant portion of his achievements in the five years between 1914 when he arrived in England and 1919 when he returned to India. Ramanujan had a startling knowledge of mathematics, mostly working out all the theories alone.[1] He made momentous advances, with his works published in many English and European journals. He was elected to the Royal Society of London in 1918.

Leaving the technical aspects of Ramanujan's achievements to those in the field of mathematics, let us focus on the story of this remarkable man, who was referred to as *The Man Who Knew Infinity* in the 2015 film based on the 1991 book by Robert Kanigel.[2] How did the journey of a young man who grew up in a remote part of India in those days take him to becoming listed among the intelligentsia of his time at such a young age? How did the Royal Society of London discover such a great mind? We should not miss this part of his story. Surprisingly, Ramanujan did not have as much formal education as his counterparts and did not obtain advanced university degrees. Yet his contributions to his life's work in mathematics was unparalleled.

At fifteen, Ramanujan read, *Synopsis of Elementary Results in Pure and Applied Mathematics, Volume 2*, written by George Shoobridge Carr. This volume contained thousands of mathematical theorems but with very brief proofs. Ramanujan spent time verifying the theorems. This helped him to discover his own inventiveness in mathematics. He went on to develop his own theorems. He secured a scholarship in 1903 to attend the University of Madras but lost his scholarship in 1904 because he focused mostly on mathematics at the expense of other subjects. This did not deter him. He continued his work without employment and living in poverty. In Ramanujan's search for permanent employment, Ramachandra Rao, a government official, interviewed him and was impressed with the young man's mathematical genius. Although Rao supported Ramanujan's research for a while, he was unwilling to live on charity and accepted a position with the Madras Port Trust instead.

Ramanujan went on to publish his first paper in the *Journal of Indian Mathematical Society* in 1911. His work gained recognition as he courageously stepped into the academic community. In 1913, he began corresponding with Godfrey H. Hardy, a British mathematician. In 1914, their relationship led to Ramanujan securing a special scholarship from the University of Madras and a grant from Trinity College, Cambridge, for Ramanujan to travel to England to further pursue his life's work. Hardy tutored him and worked with him through the years. Ramanujan made many achievements in his work during his five years in England. Unfortunately, he contracted tuberculosis in 1917. He still continued working during his fight for his life but needed to return to India in 1919 after some improvement in his condition. He later died in India in 1920. Notably, mathematicians regard Ramanujan as a genius without peer in the period after Leonhard Euler (1707-1783) and Carl Jacobi (1804-1851). In fact, long after his death, mathematicians continue to verify the unpublished results he left in his three notebooks and a pile of pages called the "lost notebook."

Thinking about the story of Ramanujan, let us try to answer a few questions. Were his incredible achievements and the respect given to his work partly or wholly due to his ingenuity? Was there a connection between his natural genius, his collaboration with peers, his opportunity to work at Trinity College, and his eventual success? Could we perhaps say the opportunity for publishing his work in India and in England was always there, but he needed to be courageous enough to try? Does it seem his opportunity to correspond with Hardy was always available, but he needed to put in the work and publish his work to make the connection? Try reading the story again and try to identify which parts of his story were related to his preparations and which parts were purely opportunities he was prepared for.

The crux of the matter is that both preparation and opportunities will meet in time. Possibly, there are many other Ramanujans out there, whose talents, skills, and ingenuity are wasting away because of a lack of opportunities for their ideas to see the light of the day. It is our responsibility to strive, to make an effort, to do what we can to make our ideas, skills, ingenuity, and life's work visible to opportunities. Ramanujan did not just sit around, working on his theorems in a corner of his home in his remote village. He stepped out into the University of Madras and into the academic community. He did incredible work and dared to publish it where other notable works were published. He initiated correspondence with his counterparts in other parts of the world. Now, history will always remember him for his contributions.

Let us consider some specific actions we can take to improve the odds of making our preparations meet with opportunities. While it is true that many opportunities in life may not be within our control or at our disposal, there are steps we can take to make our works and our lives visible to opportunities.

Open Your Work Up to Opportunities

As I mentioned earlier, opportunities abound, but our preparations must meet with them. One action we can take is to expose our work to the community of those who need it and those who make decisions about it. Please note that I suggest exposing your work and not your ideas. You want to keep certain ideas between you and only those helping you develop them until you have used the idea to produce something or solve a problem. Unless you need help from specific people to develop or advance your ideas, you should keep your ideas as part of your strategies for success. However, once you have a concrete answer for the world, it is your responsibility to open it up to opportunities by exposing it to the community of decision makers and users of what you have developed.

I will always remember my experience with my first book, *Be a Change Agent: Leadership in a Time of Exponential Change*. I put much effort into that work and verified the authenticity of every idea in the book through rigorous research and reviews. Although it was my first book, I knew it could stand side-by-side with the best books in business and represented a new voice of leadership development in the community. My challenge was that it was still my first book. Nobody knew me. I was not popular and did not have the kind of following necessary for success. I wrote to many literary agents asking them to accept and represent my work but met with disappointment with every one.

One thing I was sure of was that I wanted my work to be seen by those who need to hear the message, and I was passionate to become a successful author. I decided to keep moving forward. I hired FriesenPress to help self-publish my work. It was a wonderful experience. We ensured that everything was professionally done. We produced a book of the same or better quality of leading books published by major publishing houses, and we submitted it to Ingram to make it visible to thousands of bookshops and libraries worldwide. I hosted a book launch, publicized the work on social media, and honored invitations to speak about the work. I contacted radio stations, and a few put me on air. I told everyone I met that I had published a book. I did everything I could to make my excellent book visible.

A few weeks after publishing the book, I submitted the book to the 2021 Next Generation Indie Book Awards, the world's largest awards program for independent publishers and self-published authors as part of my effort to make the book visible to those that make literary decisions. I exposed it to scrutiny by the best literary minds and editors in the world. I was confident about the content and quality of the book, and I knew it could compete with other successful books.

That was in January 2021. While the book continued to gain some traction, I kept my hopes alive and continued executing other promotion plans, including recording an audiobook, just trying what I could to make the book visible. In May 2021, I got the good news. My book had been named winner of the gold medal for the business category of the 2021 Next Generation Indie Book Awards. This marked the beginning of tremendous exposure for the book.

Although this example may seem biased toward those who have created a product, artwork, or intellectual property, we all have personal plans and capabilities in our possession that need to be exposed to opportunities. If you do not own a business but work for an organization, how would you expose your skills, knowledge, and experience to opportunities? Many of us are conservative about our capabilities. It is okay to be modest in how we present ourselves to others, especially when in search of opportunities. However, we must find a way to ensure that the best of our work is not swept under the rug. You may need to show up when necessary, take credit for important work, step forward to take on new responsibilities that will showcase your capabilities, or discuss your skills and talents with those who make decisions at your workplace.

The point I am trying to make is that you cannot afford to do an excellent job but keep it hidden away. It is your responsibility to open your work up to opportunities. Put your name on what you achieve, shout your ideas from the rooftop, and take credit for your work. As you put effort into making significant achievements in your life's work, you should also develop a strategy for making the work visible to those who need it and those who make decisions about it. This may require that you join associations, attend conferences, go to exhibitions, set up social-media platforms, get on radio and/or TV, volunteer, develop campaigns, create marketing materials, hire a promotion specialist, host events, et cetera. Ensure that you do whatsoever you can to make your work visible. Open your work up to opportunities so it can be discovered. Allow yourself to be vulnerable and create opportunities.

Exploit Your Experience

One way to explore possibilities is to try new things. It is in trying things that we discover our own capabilities. If you have an idea and want to know whether it would work or not, you may need to conduct an experiment. One reason many people struggle in life is that they do not exploit their experience. Life is full of lessons, lessons we learn as we go through life and lessons we learn as we deliberately push ourselves into new experiences. Only by being uncomfortable do we learn. What new experience could you push yourself into that would open opportunities for you to succeed in your life's work?

I remember a client of mine, whose life's work was plumbing. He had worked as a successful plumber for a long time. In his experience as a plumber, he did not like that toilet bowls were difficult to handle during installation and repair. Just imagine carrying a new toilet bowl to install. You would need to awkwardly wrap your arms around the toilet bowl to carry that hundred-pound appliance. There is always the risk of the toilet bowl slipping from your hands or you hurting your back while carrying it.

My client decided to conduct some experiments to look for better ways to handle toilet bowls. He came up with a remarkable idea. From then on, Darrell Willim, the owner of Willim Ventures, became an inventor of an important product for the plumbing business by converting his experience into an idea and his idea into an experiment. He developed his idea until it became the Pick-Up-Stix and then commercialized the product. We worked together—collaboration—on the locking mechanism for the Pick-Up-Stix, which is now commercially available to all plumbers worldwide.

As part of your effort to explore the world of possibilities and opportunities, you may need to learn something new, such as a skill or method that you have never tried before. You may need to do something you have never done before. You may need to go somewhere you have never been before. You may need to try what you have never tried before. Do not hold back on new experiences. If you think of a new experience relevant to opening opportunities for achieving success in your life's work, do not hold back. Throw yourself into a new space and explore what you have never explored before. That experience may just be the answer to your needs and point to what you should do next to become the success you have envisioned. Or it may create an opportunity that would not have existed before.

I have seen many dreams die on arrival, dreams that did not get a chance to survive because we did not push ourselves into the experience. Sometimes we rationalize whether something would work or not, then we neglect to pursue them. One of my philosophies is that you should not say something will not work until you have tried it—and given your all. If I give you a light bulb and ask you if the light bulb still works or is dead, a way you can verify that is to find a light socket to install the bulb and flick the switch. That experiment will tell you if the bulb still works. It is the same thing with life.

When we have an idea, we must throw ourselves into experiences and use those experiences as an experiment. We must try different things out to figure out how our idea works. In fact, trying helps us to figure out how it does not work, so we can keep trying to discover how it works. Remember, only in failing do we learn to succeed. People that achieve big things are those who dared to experiment with big things. No one knows if their idea will work until they try it. We must explore possibilities for ourselves, adapt, and adjust accordingly.

Expand Your Circle

We are all only a few contacts away from those who would become the bridge from where we are to where we plan to be. You must connect people that matter with what you are trying to achieve. One way to meet people—those helpers of destiny—is by expanding your circle. You cannot afford to remain in a cocoon or stay swaddled by a few friends and family members in hopes that someone will knock on your door and present you with the fortune you have waited for. Those planning to succeed in life must be willing to expand their circle and connect with the right people.

Those planning to succeed in life must be willing to expand their circle and connect with the right people.

If you have a much less sociable personality than others or you do not have access to some platforms others have access to, that is no problem. All you need is effort and a willingness to connect with new people every time you have an opportunity to do so. Many wonderful and unexpected things happen in social gatherings such as golf clubs, events, meetings, games, and religious gatherings. You may just need to show up where people connect. The places where you meet new people do not have to be as sophisticated or specific as those I just listed. They could be anywhere as long as people are there.

In addition, do not judge people by their cover. People do not need to look like they have something for you before you connect with them. Help sometimes comes from where we least expect it. The person you could have written off may be the angel sent to you from heaven, so be open, kind, and accepting of everyone.

Connecting with people can be as simple as initiating conversations. Be sure to ask open-ended questions when you meet people for the first time so you can get to know them. Pay attention to their stories and be patient; listen to them without interruption. Be open to questions from them and be willing to share relevant information about yourself. One of my experiences while attending formal dinners is that you get to talk to everyone at the table. Even if you were not planning to offer a mini speech, someone will still at least ask for your name. Can you guess what the next question is? Of course, it's, "What do you do?" One of the best topics you can talk about is yourself. Talking about yourself in a simple and respectful way can attract people to your story.

Look at connecting with people and expanding your circle this way: people work in different areas of life, and everyone holds different pieces of a big puzzle. Imagine that your life's achievement is like a big puzzle you are trying to arrange. While working on your puzzle, you realize that there are missing pieces you do not possess, and you have many other pieces that you either do not need or can give to others. Well, that is how life works: what you need to succeed in your endeavor is in the hands of others while you hold in your hands what others need to succeed. The most successful people are those who are constantly locating all their missing pieces and arranging their puzzles at the same time giving others their puzzle pieces.

In practical terms, for example, if you are a general building contractor, you need tradespeople, among whom there may be carpenters, masons, electricians, plumbers, supervisors, and so on. You probably need an insurance broker, a lawyer, and a banker too. You need to arrange various pieces from various professions together to successfully bid on and execute a project. Some jobs may require proof you can execute a project successfully before it is awarded to you. In that case, you need to connect with all the people you need to secure and execute your building contracts. Your ability to gather the right people together for your work becomes another form of capital, without which you cannot do the work.

We need other people in our circle to help us with what we do. In the same way, other people need us to succeed in what they are doing. I have observed that people are generally willing to help or provide support to those with whom they are familiar or have close associations. Never pretend as if you do not need help. If you do, you will miss opportunities for support. Remember, John Donne taught us, "No man is an island." Certain types of support may require mutual trust, which people may not give if they do not know much about you. In other cases, we may need to trade the puzzle pieces in our hands for those missing pieces we need from others. We must be willing to connect with and work with other people in an environment of mutual respect and opportunity for everyone to succeed in what they are trying to achieve.

It is our responsibility to connect with a community of people who have the missing pieces of different puzzles and with whom we can work to improve our opportunities to succeed. Sometimes we may even need to maintain an inner core of specific individuals with whom we share a common vision and similar attitudes and discipline for achieving. In the business world, we refer to people in your inner circle as your "mastermind group," those with whom you operate at a similar frequency regarding achievements and success in life. To whom do you go to rub minds together? How could you connect with people that could support you on your journey to achievements and fulfillment in life? How would you expand your circle? Think about people at your place of work, your religious affiliation, your professional association, your sports team, your family, your friends, your customers, your community club, et cetera. Expanding your circle is one way your preparations for success in life can meet with opportunities.

Build a Team

A single tree does not make a forest. Show me someone who attained a great achievement in life or became successful in business, and I will show you their team. No one singlehandedly builds an edifice. We do greater things when we come together, when we employ our collective effort and synergize our efforts to do what no individual can do. If you are serious about achieving something significant and notable, you must consider building a team around your vision.

> *No one singlehandedly builds an edifice. We do greater things when we come together, when we employ our collective effort and synergize our efforts to do what no individual can do.*

Why do you think the military is arranged into squads, platoons, battalions, legions, and so on? The formations of ants and the patterns in which they organize themselves has continued to be a subject of study by humans. They are a splendid example of teamwork. A lone ant will not build an anthill, but a team will. Both the military and the ants know the size of the problem or achievement and the size of the group are dependent on each other. The power of synergy cannot be substituted by skill, expertise, or experience.

One elementary school math topic is word problems. In word problems, we tackle questions such as, "If it takes five hours for a person to complete a job, how many hours would it take two people to complete the same job?" How did you answer that question? Two and a half hours? That was the simplistic approach to the question as our teachers taught us. The question assumes there are two people working independent of one another, whereas the true idea of two people doing the job was for them to work together as a team. Thinking they are two independent workers denies one of the most important principles of success: the power of teamwork. Most of us are unable to multiply our success because we see additional people as separate.

> *When we come together as a team, the team's overall effort is not the sum of the effort of the individuals working on the team. It is **multiples** of the efforts of the individuals.*

But here is how synergy works. When we come together as a team, the team's overall effort is not the sum of the effort of the individuals working on the team. It is *multiples* of the efforts of the individuals. That is exactly why farmers used yokes to tie two animals together to drive a plow. If the farmer used each animal individually and combined their effort, much less work would be done than when they are yoked together. That is synergy. Synergy helps multiply success through collective capacity. Those who are successful take advantage of this principle. They recruit the best people onto their teams and encourage them to work together in synergy.

Remember, no one singlehandedly achieves greatness. You need a team to drive your vision forward. If you plan to achieve something important in your lifetime, be ready to bring other people onto your team to work with you in synergy. One more thing to note is that everyone's gifts, talents, and abilities are different. Others will fill the gaps where you are not gifted. Do not struggle to do it all. Build a team. Give yourself an opportunity to thrive, achieve remarkable things, and become a person of significance by building a team around your dream.

Push Your Personal Boundaries

The only boundaries we should not push are those set by principles, such as those set by nature. Every other boundary is movable. To have opportunities to achieve tremendous success, we need to push our personal boundaries, expand our borders, and press into new territories. Unless we keep pushing the boundaries, we will soon find that our capacity for reaching personal goals will begin to plateau. There should be no cap placed on our ability to do significant things in life. There should be no limit to what we can achieve.

One of the ways to become a lifetime achiever is to develop the discipline needed for pushing personal boundaries. Many successful athletes understand this principle. To receive a gold medal at the Olympics, you need to push your personal boundaries to compete with a host of others and win. If your goal is to beat an existing athletic record, you must continue to push yourself until you are able to achieve the feat.

Part of the issue with many of us is that we settle into a particular level of success, having forgotten that our previous success sets a bar for us to overcome the next time. We should not allow past success to stop us from attaining further success. Neither should we allow past failure to prevent us from moving forward. We must continue to push many personal boundaries. These include knowledge and skills, financial and economic, career and life's work, health and fitness, relationship and network, and personal vision boundaries. Let us examine the knowledge and skills boundary as an example. We discussed earlier that knowledge is power. Your ability to push your knowledge and skills boundary will determine how much you can add value to yourself. We stop growing the day we stop learning. Think about your current level of knowledge and skills. Can you push that boundary? Pushing your knowledge boundary may require you to read new books, enroll in a course, obtain a certificate or degree, join a discussion group, learn a new method of doing your work, or practice a skill. The only real limits are those that we place on ourselves through our imagination.

> *Our previous success sets a bar for us to overcome the next time.*

It is in overcoming boundaries that we break forth into new opportunities. Let your preparation meet with opportunities as you break barriers and set the stage for you to thrive in the world of opportunities.

CHAPTER 7 DISCOVERY QUESTIONS

1. List three specific actions you can take within the next week to make your work visible to those who need it and/or those who make decisions about your area of work.

2. What new experience could you push yourself to that would open opportunities for you to succeed in your life's work, career, or undertaking? Is there somewhere you can go or something you can learn?

3. Where would you find new people to expand your circle? How often do you connect with new people at conferences, learning events, social events, work, and on social media?

4. Building a team around your vision is important for success. What qualities would you like to see in your team members? Where would you find people with those qualities, and how would you connect with them?

5. Which of the boundaries mentioned in the section on pushing personal boundaries do you think you need to push at this time? What next steps can you take in pushing the boundary?

CHAPTER 8

UNDERSTAND THE SEASONS

To everything there is a season, a time for every purpose under heaven.

~ The Bible[1] ~

When the winds of change blow, remember ... sometimes what appears dead is simply preparing for a new season.

~ Jane Lee Logan ~

I came across a documentary written by Stephen J. Mraz and published in *Machine Design* on October 27, 2020. It was a brief history of the Boeing 747 jumbo jet.[2] Boeing rolled out the first 747 in Everett, Washington, in 1968 after 29 months of work by over 4,500 engineers. It was the world's largest commercial airplane until 2007 at 64-feet tall and with a wingspan of 196 feet. The plane made its first flight on February 9, 1969.[3] Eventually, the number of airplanes built totaled 1,558.

This remarkable plane was powered by four engines, which Boeing sourced from various jet engine manufacturers including Pratt and Whitney, Rolls Royce, and GE. The Boeing 747 even provided enough room to accommodate a second level of seats, with the upper deck having the floor space of an entire Boeing 737. With the capacity to accommodate more than 500 people onboard, the total number of passengers that have flown aboard the plane is about half the population of our planet, or 3.5 billion.

The 747 served a variety of purposes: military command centers, space-shuttle carriers, airborne tankers for refueling jets, and Dreamlifter cargo planes. In fact, two 747s became the US presidents' planes: Air Force One.

They even thought to use it as an airborne aircraft carrier, to convert it so could carry up to ten small jets that would be airlifted to where they were needed, launched, refueled, and recovered. This idea, though technically feasible, was jettisoned because of the many risks involved. Nevertheless, the Boeing 747 airplane became a significant landmark in the history of aircraft manufacturing and flight.

As remarkable as the Boeing 747 airplane was, it is now retired. Mraz put it this way, "The Queen of the Skies flies into the sunset." Its season is over. Airlines all over the world have put their 747 jumbo jets in retirement homes, never to fly again. It is now the season of more efficient planes: the newer, smaller, smarter airliners. The emergence of the 747 in 1968 was a revolutionary beginning, the season for a game-changing airliner. However, the season lasted only about fifty years. It did not last forever. It is now the season of new and more efficient airliners that meet modern-day requirements and business models. Surely, seasons change. As seasons always change, always be ready with new ideas and new successes.

Nature Is a Teacher

Nature has arranged events as they occur in seasons and cycles. The cyclical events follow the fundamental laws of nature. No one denies the principles that guide seasonal changes. In fact, we base our lives on the seasons. After every winter, we expect spring, and we are sure another summer and fall will follow. We depend on the seasons for farming, construction, sports, travel, fishing, and more. Our schools follow seasonal calendars. We know seasons come and go.

It is apparent that the way physical laws govern cyclical physical events is the same way certain principles guide the cycles humans experience on their life's journey. With family life, for example, you may say there are four seasons: singleness, marriage, raising children, and becoming empty nesters. You may also say there are four seasons in one's life, including childhood, youth, adulthood, and old age. "Every stage of life has its own form of power, and we're always sort of terrified as to whether we can make the jump to the next form of power," journalist and novelist Chuck Palahniuk explains for us. It is true that we must harness the best of every season of life and enjoy every moment as we evolve into the person we are meant to be.

> *We may not choose the seasons of life that we experience, but we can change how we experience the seasons of life by focusing on the seasons of personal leadership.*

So, while there are seasons of nature and seasons of life, so too are there seasons of personal leadership. We do not have any control over physical seasons, but we can alter the course of our own lives. We may not choose the seasons of life that we experience, but we can change how we experience the seasons of life by focusing on the seasons of personal leadership. The seasons of personal leadership primarily relate to how one will respond to life's circumstances and changes to alter, deliberately, the course of their life.

One major difference between the seasons of personal leadership and other seasons of life is that they do not depend on one's physical age or cycle of life, but on personal preparation and opportunities as discussed in the previous chapter. There could be two individuals at the same season or stage of life but at different seasons of personal leadership. It is also possible to have someone advanced in age just starting their journey to personal leadership. As such, there are five seasons of personal leadership.

The Five Seasons of Personal Leadership

1. The conditioning season: developing the mindset of success

I have noticed that the first thing that happens to people who embark upon a pursuit of personal leadership is a shift in the way they think. Developing the mindset of success and personal achievement is the first season of personal leadership. This season is largely dependent on one's readiness to influence the course and experiences of their life, deliberately. As I mentioned earlier, to reach the summit of Mount Everest, you must first see conquering the mountain in your mind. The way we think has a profound impact on how our lives turn out.

> *To reach the summit of Mount Everest, you must first see conquering the mountain in your mind. The way we think has a profound impact on how our lives turn out.*

The environment your mind is exposed to and the conditions of your mind shape the thinking pattern that eventually becomes your mindset and consequent experience. Mind conditioning has to do with what you believe about yourself in relation to your personal pursuit of success and achievement and is the result of the bank of information residing in your subconscious mind. If your subconscious mind is filled with negative thoughts, impossibilities, failure, disappointments, or not enough ambition, you will find it difficult to begin a journey to success. Those conditioned to take a back seat or come second to others based on their upbringing, training, experience, or miseducation will find it difficult to begin a personal journey of achievement.

The remedy for negative mind conditioning is to replace old beliefs with new beliefs through deliberate exposure to the new information necessary to develop the mindset of success and fortify the mind against negative beliefs. To deliberately expose oneself to positive beliefs may require a change of association and a change of internal language. Associating with those who share positive perspectives on life will influence you to start thinking similarly. This association may or may not be physical or in-person. As discussed earlier, we can learn much from others through their works: books, media, et cetera. In addition, what we profess with our mouths is a reflection of what is deep down inside us. For our internal language to change, we must change the content of our thoughts and our imagination. We must continuously meditate, think, and rethink about new, positive information and beliefs. Shift your focus from seeing things the way they are to seeing things the way they could be, positively. Replace your "I can't" with "I can." Replace "impossible" with "I'm possible." The information and knowledge in this book provide a great platform to recondition your mind for success. Most successful people start their journey to success by developing their mindset for success. Rarely does one ever innately possess a mindset for success.

This conditioning season is the season when achievers develop a sense of personal agency—or the mindset you directly influence your own life with—believe in their potential, develop the desire to do something meaningful, nurture ambitions, and dream of achieving significant things. It is a season when we dream big and make the decision to head out into the unknown, trying to answer questions as we go along and grounding ourselves in the belief that our lives will count for something important and meaningful. It is a season when we question where we are and begin to think of where we could be.

In this first season of personal leadership, we resolve to pursue our personal purpose and release our potential. It seems this season does not really end, in reality, but rather creates the foundation for the beginning of great achievements in life.

2. The planning season: developing the toolset for success

Developing the mindset of success causes you to take action, any action that will shape your ability to become a great achiever. If you ask successful farmers, they will tell you one secret of their success is understanding they must plan during winter. In this season, the farmer plans for planting, ensuring that there are seeds, machinery, and tools, et cetera needed for planting, managing growth, and harvesting. It is usually a time of preparation for both known and unforeseen circumstances.

The planning season of personal leadership is when we develop the toolset for success. It is a time of investing in personal growth and development. It is a time of spending what we must to gain what we need for success. It is a time of grooming and sharpening. It is a time when we shape our character, attitude, aptitude, and inner strength for what is to come. It is a time to develop the self-discipline and the resilience it takes to become and remain an achiever. It is a time to acquire the skills and know-how for what we envision and for the direction in which we shall go.

During the planning season, we learn to overcome obstacles and grow through the smaller wins. Achievements come in varying sizes. No one who has not learned to manage smaller achievements and sizable personal successes can expect to launch something significant and expect success. The time of plucking low-hanging fruit presents us with an opportunity to learn and grow into bigger things in life. The biblical King David rescued sheep by fighting and killing a lion and a bear before conquering the giant Goliath that threatened his country.

This stage of personal leadership is integral. If you do not have the tool-set for success, you will be limited in how far you can go or become unable to sustain success when it comes. Those who go

> *No one who has not learned to manage smaller achievements and sizable personal successes can expect to launch something significant and expect success.*

through this stage early enough in life may be fortunate. However, as I mentioned earlier, the seasons of personal leadership have little to do with the stage of life. Anyone can learn to prepare for great achievements at any stage of life.

3. The launching season: deploying ideas and releasing potential

The reality of life is that planning and preparing give way to opportunities, just as winter gives way to spring. The essence of preparation is simply the actual doing of what one has planned. The launching season is a time of planting: the time of working on dreams and implementing ideas. It a season when we do what we have always wanted to do. It is a season of action. No one should ever expect to harvest anything without first planting their seeds. During the planting season, we put the seeds in the ground, water the soil, and take care of the plants as they grow. Sometimes we need to ensure that the stakes holding the plants are stable and secure. We may need to remove weeds and protect the growing plants. We continually invest resources, effort, and time in the plants in anticipation of their maturity.

Literally speaking, the launching season is a time when we grow our businesses or careers or whatever else our life's endeavor is. This is when we begin by implementing our ideas and directing our potential toward achieving something significant in life. During this season, we put a lot of effort into succeeding in whatsoever we do. We use all our energy and invest ourselves into our endeavor. This is the most uncertain season of all as it comes with a lot of risk-taking. This season tests the validity and authenticity of ideas. This is when we discover if those ideas and dreams might germinate and produce plants that can be nurtured into maturity.

The good thing about the planting season is that once the seeds germinate and grow, we get to see everything blossom. Everything comes to life, and we relish seeing our plants grow. It feels immensely satisfying when we begin to fulfill a dream or implement an idea. There is a sense of meaning that we derive from putting effort into achieving something of value and significance. The launching season is a time when we realize the dignity of labor and the joy of aspiring to succeed on a worthwhile course.

During this season, we also have to be wary. Crops can be attacked by bugs, diseases, animals, hailstorms, fire, et cetera, and the farmer needs to protect the crops against those external forces. In the same way, we need to be on guard and ensure that we never stop working to protect our work during the launching season. We must ensure that the environment is conducive to productivity that will eventually result in copious yields.

The launching season of personal leadership is a critical season as it comes and goes swiftly. It is a window of opportunity. What you sow during this time is what you will harvest in the next season. If you sow little by putting minimal effort into your life's endeavor, prepare for a lean harvest. But if you diligently work during this season, bearing the pain,

> *If you sow little by putting minimal effort into your life's endeavor, prepare for a lean harvest.*

standing resolute in the face of tough times, enduring the difficulties, keeping your head above water, and giving your all, you will be in a better position to realize a bountiful harvest.

4. The season of significance: becoming the success you envisioned

You may remember this statement from the beginning of this book: "The world must make room for a person who has discovered, and has the desire and determination, to develop and exploit their gifts, talents, and abilities to establish themselves in what they have determined to be their exact purpose and calling in life." The season of significance is the season of personal leadership when we actualize our dreams of becoming a person who has attained notable success. It is a season of harvest. Every planting season is succeeded by harvest season. The harvest is a time of abundance.

When you see people doing well for themselves in their life's work, reaping an abundance of wealth, recognition, notoriety, personal achievements, awards and accolades, public honors, or personal fulfillment, remember that they have most likely passed through the preceding seasons. Achievements can be big or small, but no matter how small an achievement may be, no one realizes anything of value at zero cost. The season of significance is the time when we realize the results of our efforts. During this time, we attract respect from others. People acknowledge us for who we have become because of our resolve and determination to succeed.

Meanwhile, the definition of success and life achievements may be relative, depending on one's worldview, the size of one's dream, or the type of one's endeavor. For example, graduating from college or university is an achievement. Growing a business to a desired size and profitability is an achievement. Winning or being nominated for a Grammy Award is an achievement. Building or buying a house is an achievement. Fulfilling a desire to contribute a certain amount of money to a charity of choice is an achievement. Getting back on your feet after an illness is an achievement. You can add to the unending list; anything you work hard to attain and finally accomplish is an achievement.

We must realize that achievements come in levels and sizes. There is no one perfect definition of personal achievement and success. There is no one-size-fits-all definition. The most important thing is for everyone to strive to maximize whatsoever gifts, talent, and opportunities we have in life. The true measure of success is how much you achieve in relation to how much you began with. Did you plant all your seeds? Did you maximize your potential? Did you work to the best of your ability? Ask yourself at the end of each day, "Was that the best I could do?" Ask yourself at the beginning of each day, "What is the best I could give to my life's work today that will yield an abundance and become a source of blessing to the world and personal fulfillment for me in the season of significance?"

> *The true measure of success is how much you achieve in relation to how much you began with.*

5. The season of meaning and fulfillment: making the world a better place for all

Back at the beginning of the book, I averred that the purpose of a thing is to meet a need outside of that thing and that your life's purpose is unlikely to be centered upon you. For example, financial wealth is a good thing, and if you can, make all the money you have the ability to make. However, the true purpose of making large sums of money is not for self-aggrandizement. Just look around you and see how miserable it can be to have all the money in the world and no sense of personal fulfillment, happiness, and meaning. The richest people are not necessarily the most fulfilled people. Why do you think many of the richest people eventually give away their wealth to charity? You may need to think deeply about that.

No one, and I really mean no one, can have a true sense of meaning in life until they start living for something greater, for something beyond themselves. There is always a season of life when you ask yourself repeatedly, "And so what?" You reached the pinnacle of your dreams and now ask, "And so what?" The season of meaning and fulfillment is one we should dive into as early as possible in life. There is no point waiting to go through all the other seasons of personal leadership before experiencing

No one, and I really mean no one, can have a true sense of meaning in life until they start living for something greater, for something beyond themselves.

this season. You can work to achieve fulfillment from step one. And as your life evolves into something greater, you can find greater and greater opportunities to become a person of substance to others and society. The season of giving back to others, contributing to society, and making the world a better place is the time when we derive real meaning from life.

Guiding Principles for the Seasons

Here are five characteristic principles that guide the seasons of personal leadership.

1. There is no universality of seasons

The seasons of personal leadership are not universal. People living in the same geographic region experience the same physical weather conditions and the same physical seasonal cycles. However, the seasons of personal leadership are different for everyone. Your seasons are tailor-made for you. Your life is unique to you. No one can live your life, and you cannot live anyone else's life. Your readiness, planning, and opportunities generally dictate the seasons of personal leadership you will experience. Everyone goes through the seasons of personal leadership differently to achieve an end specific to you.

2. There is no permanence of seasons

Seasons change; therefore, everyone must brace for change. No season lasts forever no matter the circumstances surrounding it. The season will surely change because seasons are cyclic. Every season is only a window of opportunities. Note that even the season of fulfillment—when we experience the most success and personal achievement—does not last forever. This concept applies to every area of life. That is why everyone must make the best use of every opportunity in life. In the same way, failures and challenges do not last forever. They appear within the cycles of the seasons. You should focus on your stability and your ability to overcome obstacles. Be patient. Focus on the prize. You cannot afford to give up hope in the face of problems. Get comfortable with change. There is no permanence of seasons.

3. There is no set timeline for seasons

How long one experiences the full cycle of the seasons of personal leadership depends on the particular endeavor and one's pace. A redwood tree may need many centuries to attain full maturity whereas an apple tree may take ten years. Everyone goes through the seasons of personal leadership with different timelines for different purposes. Your particular pursuit and your personal pace determine how long you spend in the cycle of the seasons. The time and effort it takes to complete a college education is different from the time and effort it takes to repair a bicycle. Each undertaking requires different amounts of planning and effort and different amounts of time for each person. There is no set timeline for the seasons of personal leadership.

4. Seasons can be altered

Unlike the natural seasons, the seasons of personal leadership can be altered. One can lengthen or shorten any particular season through their actions or lack of actions. One of the most important lessons to take away from this book is that anyone can alter the course of their life through what they believe and what they do. Our lives are not out of control but under control. Everyone chooses how to respond to life. You may not choose things that happen external to you, but you have the capacity to choose how you respond to your experiences.

5. Every season teaches us a lesson

One way to improve our lives is to learn from our experiences at every stage of life. What we experience through the seasons of personal leadership presents us with opportunities to iterate our actions as we implement the lessons learned. Sometimes things do not turn out exactly as we would have expected. But we can make sense of a season that seems not to make sense if we adopt a bigger-picture approach. Our lives are not as segmented as we usually think. Everything is interconnected, and when we zoom out and connect the dots, we can see beyond a singular situation; our stories begin to make sense, and we can see opportunities that lie ahead.

CHAPTER 8 DISCOVERY QUESTIONS

1. What season or stage of life are you currently in? Child-hood, youth, adulthood, or old age? Focusing on the pos-itives, mention five things that are unique and worth celebrating about your stage of life.

2. Going back to the five seasons of personal leadership, what season are you in? Does it seem like you are in more than one season at a time, depending on what you are trying to achieve?

3. In your opinion, which of the five seasons of personal leadership is generally the most important? Why do you think so? Which is the most important to you?

4. Using the guiding principles, we learned that there is no universality of the seasons of personal leadership. How does that make you feel? Do you feel unique and encour-aged to keep moving forward? If not, why?

5. Think about a season you have gone through. Write five lessons you learned during that season.

CHAPTER 9

BECOME A ROLE MODEL

It's my responsibility to help others, to be a positive example. I want to be a role model for others, to help others like me get a chance.

~ Rob Jeter ~

Leaders inspire others to become better at learning, doing, growing, and becoming.

~ Dele Ola ~

L ong did I contemplate the title of this chapter. Should it be "Become a Role Model" or "Become a Leader," I wondered? Well, a real leader is a role model: a person of influence and value. Real leaders reproduce themselves, building other leaders and showing others how to become successful. There is a serious deficiency of real leadership in our world today. Most people tend to look for leadership in the wrong places, thinking that people who have some kind of positional authority, political or economic power, or have attained a level of personal success are automatically able to provide leadership. There are people who parade themselves as leaders but lack the character, attributes, and attitudes of real leaders.

Let me provide a bit of context here. Leadership is first personal-focused before people-focused. For one to lead others, they must first successfully lead themselves. Becoming someone others should follow, a role model, calls for personal awareness, personal discovery, personal development, and personal sacrifices. Your leadership starts within your niche, including how you harness whatsoever you possess in the form of gifts, talents, skills, and personal abilities. How you pursue personal growth and strive to become a better person is one of the most important components of your ability to influence others. You cannot lead or inspire others before first doing the work yourself. Words are but empty vessels without action. People will see right through you and turn to a true leader. Once you've done your work—built your foundations, created your teams, exploited your creativity, explored possibilities, and established your life's work—then you've reached the pinnacle and must use all you've learned to help others achieve their successes.

> *How you pursue personal growth and strive to become a better person is one of the most important components of your ability to influence others.*

The truth is that until we begin to influence others positively through what we do in our life's work and other activities, the cycle of our successes in life is not complete. One way to leave a permanent footprint on earth is to reproduce success in others, giving them an opportunity to thrive and showing them the way. Yes, leaders *are* role models, showing others how to pursue their personal leadership and succeed in a world that gives nothing to anyone on a platter of gold.

I met Fred Doern for the first time in 2009 during the opening reception of the Centre for Aerospace Technology and Training (CATT), a partnership between StandardAero and Manitoba's premier polytechnic institute, Red River College Polytechnic.

Fred was the chair of the mechanical and manufacturing program at the college, and I was attending the University of Manitoba's graduate school. I attended the event as a member of the innovation community and sat in on the sessions, watching as stakeholders of the partnership mounted the podium and delivered their presentations.

Fred's presentation was one I will always remember as it related directly to my work at the university. It reinforced my conviction that there was a future for my career within the local aerospace and manufacturing community. I thought Fred's attendance was a highlight of the event; he commanded much attention. Although I did not meet him one-to-one, it was as if my thoughts vibrated at the same frequency as Fred's thoughts as I listened to him speak from the lectern and during the facility tours. The event ended, but I kept copies of the presentations and contact information. I even repeatedly reread the information about the event on the CD we all received.

Three years later, in 2012, Fred and his colleagues at the college were expanding their research program and opening the Technology Access Centre for Aerospace and Manufacturing (TACAM) after securing additional grants from the federal government and the local aerospace industry. Fortuitously, they needed a new researcher to help develop the aerospace research portfolio and serve as the college's resident engineer at the CATT. And just a day before the job posting was to close, my friend, Dotun Akinlade, contacted me and told me about the job. I was not looking for a job then because I was ramping up my doctoral research work. But when I saw the advertisement, I knew the opportunity was for me; it lined up with my personal vision of how the next stage of my career would unfold.

Needless to say, I joined Fred's team in May 2012, in what became a rewarding and uplifting career move for me. Knowing and working with Fred is one of the most impactful experiences I have had in my career. It is not an overstatement to say that Fred found me, invested in me, and set me up for success in Canada's applied research space. During our four solid years of working together, he showed me how to become successful, provided all the support I needed, and introduced me to everyone that mattered within the innovation community. I learned how to think like an innovator, drive important partnerships, work across technical disciplines, attract large financial resources, lead teams, and develop confidence. I will never forget many of the occasions when Fred introduced me as his colleague at important meetings and gave me the chance to rise as a star while he cheered me on. He presented me to the community as someone who could become a true leader.

As a result, I got the opportunity to lead the growing team at the TACAM when Fred retired in 2016. In fact, he trusted me with his vision to establish a smart factory in Winnipeg. After his retirement, I worked with internal and external stakeholders, leaders, and the government to finally actualize this vision in 2019. Fred, alongside his colleague, Don McDonald, Dean of Transportation, Aviation, and Manufacturing; and my former supervisor, Ray Hoemsen, the executive director of the research enterprise, inspired and supported me on my journey into organizational leadership. They are role models indeed: people who took a personal interest in showing others the way and ensuring others attained a level of success that equaled and surpassed theirs. The world needs more people like Fred, Don, and Ray, who give of themselves to equip others for success.

In my journey through the wins and shortfalls of life, I found that becoming a role model and giving others the opportunity to succeed is the most rewarding and fulfilling part of the pursuit of personal leadership. Let me take you through some of the lessons

I have learned from my own experiences and from my relationships with other real leaders over the years. Here are the attributes of role models we should all emulate.

Role Models Exemplify Success and Personal Achievements

If you conduct a quick search on people the world refers to as role models, you will find they are people who have attained a significant level of personal success. You may come across lists of respected individuals like Oprah Winfrey, Steve Jobs, and Nelson Mandela. While they are truly role models, I do not want us to confuse role modeling with fame. Not all famous people are real leaders or role models. However, one thing all role models have in common is that they have gone ahead of others. In some cases, they have achieved things *before* others, while in other cases, they have achieved *more* than others. Going ahead of others may also mean taking the lead or showing personal responsibility for others. Nevertheless, the opportunity to be a role model may present itself at any stage of personal development and/or personal success. We become better at role modeling success and increase our capacity to influence others as we build on existing experiences and achieve greater levels of success.

Although no particular level of success is required to be a role model, it is clear people look up to those who have something to offer. Therefore, role models should exemplify success and personal achievement, so others are likely to gravitate to them. Becoming an example of success that people can follow is an effective way to influence others. People want to listen to those who have traveled the same road they are trying to travel.

Exemplifying success gives us a platform for influencing others, giving them an opportunity to follow our lead. A person role modeling personal leadership should be an example of visionary thinking, diligence, resilience, collaboration, humility, and constant pursuit of excellence. Those experiencing continual success are more likely to have people looking to them for guidance, mentoring, coaching, or assistance. Our personal achievements open doors for us to share our experiences with others, and we need to accept that responsibility.

> *Becoming an example of success that people can follow is an effective way to influence others. People want to listen to those who have traveled the same road they are trying to travel.*

The key is to let whom we have become work for others by deliberately exemplifying personal achievement. This is not synonymous with flaunting one's success and wealth or becoming arrogant or condescending. A seemingly successful but unnecessarily haughty individual cannot deceive followers for long. True role modeling is about actions, not words. That is why our personal successes must be married with character, so others can freely grant us the authority to personally influence the shaping of their own lives for success.

Role Models Must Develop Positive Character

Steven R. Covey said,

> I believe leadership lies more in character than in technical competence, but these two are interwoven. As people grow in competence, they gain awareness of a new dimension of their character. Then, as they begin to develop that aspect of their character, they find that their competence also increases.[1]

Your character is a reflection of your values and moral judgment. Your character is more important than your charisma. One

can be talented but lack character. Your beliefs and repeated behaviors determine your character, and your background, associations, exposure, experiences, and personal choices shape your
beliefs, behaviors, and eventually your character. It is your character traits that show your true nature. You cannot separate yourself from your character.

The way to sustain success and achievement—and continually receive support from patrons, friends, family, and associates—is to develop positive character. Without character built on
a foundation of positive values and sound moral judgment, we
are unable to develop the trust needed to stand unequivocally as
role models. A real leader or role model exemplifies character,
both to those close to
them and to those watch-
ing from afar.

Of course, no one is
perfect, and we are all
susceptible to errors and
mistakes. However, to
become a role model of
all-round success, you

*Without character built on a
foundation of positive values and
sound moral judgment, we are
unable to develop the trust
needed to stand unequivocally as
role models.*

must embrace integrity, which is the most important quality of
trust and positive character. A person of integrity is not without
flaws but constantly, without compromise, exhibits the fundamental belief and practice of honesty and truthfulness. People of
integrity are truthful about their weaknesses and strengths and
are not afraid to reveal how human they are, just like everyone
else, despite their achievements and successes in life.

In a world that continues to advance in every field but continues to experience a decline in moral standards and a serious ero-
sion of positive societal values, we need real leaders to model the

character and inner strength needed to build and sustain our successes. A successful person without positive character can be likened to the biblical Samson, who possessed great strength but lacked the character to sustain his role in leading a nation. Your personal integrity, and your character, will protect you and empower you to model success and personal achievement.

As I mentioned earlier, our character must be built on a positive value system and sound moral judgment. Here are some values a role model should consider as building blocks for their character.[2]

- embracing honesty in all situations
- considering both the common good and the greater good
- placing value on both human lives and animal lives
- developing a sense of respect for oneself and others
- treating both public and private property and infrastructure with respect
- cultivating goodwill toward others and actively seeking to eradicate inequality and barriers to full participation in society for all
- becoming a steward of the resources on our planet and elsewhere within human reach

Role Models Influence Others to Act

Being a role model does not mean being a lone star. Real role models don't just roar and show off their prowess and let the world know that a person of impeccable character has arrived. Real role models have both the intention and the determination to incite others to action. After all, the purpose of role modeling is to influence others to become better people, change their course, reinforce their effort, or start on a journey. To become a role model requires us to be deliberate in inspiring others through our actions, thereby helping them take action.

There are many ways to become deliberate when working to develop others. You can mentor, coach, teach, or share, whether you are compensated for it or not. It is even possible to influence others to act without any contact or personal knowledge of someone. Many have achieved this by sharing their experiences and ideas through podcasts, radio shows, TV spots, public speeches, training classes, books, and more. There is no point keeping your success formula to yourself. Be generous in the way you share success tips with others; be deliberate.

Thankfully, there are already some who have taken it upon themselves to provide direct encouragement, support, advice, and more to people to help them grow and take their places as achievers. Just think about those around you. What can you do to lift someone up? Do you have the opportunity at your place of work, in your business, or in your class to inspire someone through what you say and do to also give them the opportunity to thrive? I am a product of direct inspiration from other achievers who told me and showed me that I could become whoever I have determined to become in life.

Role Models Use Resources to Build Others

Some role models have the opportunity to relate directly with those they influence. Knowing those emulating you and striving to achieve success based on your principles offers a tremendous advantage when you are trying to help them succeed. It allows you to use the resources you've amassed to build others. Remember, it is a great privilege for you to contribute to the growth, development, and preparation of others for success. Be generous with your money, time, possessions, and knowledge.

One of the most expensive resources you can give to someone is your time. The time you spend showing others the way is invaluable. An old Chinese proverb says, "If you want one year of prosperity, grow grains. If you want ten years of prosperity, grow trees. If you want one hundred years of prosperity, grow people." There is no way we can grow people without investing time in them. If you are a business owner or a manager who does not grow your people, you will soon reach a ceiling and eventually wither away. You will miss the opportunity to increase your prosperity by developing your people. One thing that guarantees long lasting prosperity is the development of people. Human capital is the most important resource on earth, and we build this capital when we invest in other people.

A major reason to invest in others is to give them a head start in life. People do not need to make the same mistakes you made while on your journey to achieving. Giving people a head start is not the same as denying them an opportunity to learn through their experiences. It just means they can start at a higher level and go further than they would have without help. Other people do not need to suffer as you did. Support those around you who are making genuine efforts to become achievers.

Giving people a head start is not the same as denying them an opportunity to learn through their experiences. It just means they can start at a higher level and go further than they would have without help.

In certain instances, we just need to give back to the system that supported us. I cherish those who establish foundations, open charities, set up endowments and scholarships, volunteer to serve in organizations, and give of their personal resources for others in the spirit of genuine care and contribution to humanity. Giving back is a wonderful way to be a role model of success for others. We shall learn more about this in the next chapter.

A Role Model Can Become a Bridge for Others

As I wrap up this chapter, I would like you to think about this question. What could you do for others that they would not be able to do for themselves? Sometimes, achieving tremendous success just requires a little help from someone to help us traverse a gap. As I mentioned in chapter seven, you are only a few contacts away from those who could become the bridge from where you are to where you plan to be. The reality is that you too may just be the bridge someone else needs to traverse a gap.

Although this does not sound like a *required* attribute of a role model, a role model is one who not only leads with words and personal achievements, but also with good deeds, helping others to connect with the much-needed opportunity to succeed. In many cases, all we need to do is connect people with one another, make an introduction, provide a reference, write a word of praise, patronize someone, provide a platform, or stand in the gap for others.

One important thing to remember is that those you did not help today, who are determined to reach their goals anyway, will find help somewhere else tomorrow. How will they look at you, how will they see you once they've found their own success elsewhere? How excel-

> *Those you did not help today, who are determined to reach their goals anyway, will find help somewhere else tomorrow.*

lent would it be for you to see those whom you have helped to overcome obstacles become the success they envisioned? How satisfying would that be? Do not only *preach* to others, show them by becoming a bridge for others.

CHAPTER 9 DISCOVERY QUESTIONS

1. In your personal journey, who is that one person that has influenced you the most? Why did the person have such an influence on you? What do you like most about the person?

2. In what ways have you been or are you trying to become a role model to others? How could you exemplify success and achievements for those you are influencing? Why should they follow you?

3. Write down five positive character traits you need to be an effective role model for others. What behaviors can hamper your followers' view of you?

4. List three activities you can personally do to influence others to act. How can you get someone to act based on your influence?

5. Take a moment to think deeply. Is there someone for whom you could become a bridge? What specific thing could you do for them to move them from where they are to where they would like to be?

CHAPTER 10

LEAVE A LEGACY

If you would not be forgotten as soon as you are dead, either write something worth reading, or do something worth writing.

~ Benjamin Franklin ~

A good name [earned by honorable behavior, godly wisdom, moral courage, and personal integrity] is more desirable than great riches; And favor is better than silver and gold.

~ The Bible[1] ~

What is your story? I have used the stories of many people to highlight key points throughout this book. I carefully chose each story for what it represents. The stories speak of their legacies. Everyone leaves a story behind whether written or not. People will remember you for who you were and what you did. Your footprint becomes a legacy after leaving a place or an assignment. In broader terms, you will leave your footprint in the world when you are gone.

As such, this footprint could be positively momentous, or it could be inconsequential or disreputable. Not every legacy is good. A good legacy is left largely by choice. We can purposefully construct how people will remember us. Yes, we can write a story with our lives that will remain long after we are gone. How can we do that? By deliberately introducing what will become our legacies into our everyday life. The reason many people's lives become unremarkable is because they were not deliberate in leaving a legacy. If you want people to remember you for something, then do it deliberately. People will remember your deeds, whether good or bad.

There is no need to wait for an opportunity or to attain a level of success before thinking and acting on your legacies. As long as you are alive, now is the time to think, plan, and act on your legacies. Do not say you will start that orphanage when you are retired. Do not say you will write that book when you are eighty. Do not let spending time with your family or raising your children become your smallest priority because of your job. If you can think of a good deed, go ahead and do it. Do not wait for a *convenient* time to do that which you would like people to remember you for. There is no perfect time in that sense. Let your priority be that which will last long after you go.

> *If you can think of a good deed, go ahead and do it. Do not wait for a* convenient *time to do that which you would like people to remember you for.*

I was sitting in my office sometime in 2019 when one of my colleagues came in to discuss a work-related challenge about relating with colleagues from other departments. While coming up with suggestions on how to deal with the matter, I reminded my colleague that I was sitting in a chair that someone else sat in, many years earlier, and that someone else would sit in the same chair when I was gone. I did not mean the literal chair but that I was not going to be the team leader forever. I remembered clearly the legacy of the people that had led the team before me, and I became cognizant of the legacy that I too would leave behind when someone else occupied my position. That perspective helped us determine how to respond to the situation. People will remember how you treated them.

One of the principles we learned in this book is that there is no permanence of seasons. It breaks my heart to see people in positions of authority using or misusing their power and forgetting their possible legacies, legacies that could tell of indiscretion and irresponsibility. We could think of many people who have left legacies of tyranny, selfishness, betrayal, destruction, nepotism, racism, crime, and more. We have seen the rich oppress the poor and the fortunate ridicule those less privileged. Those are not good legacies to leave behind, no matter the degree of one's success.

Though legacies can come in many forms, here are seven of the most common.

Seven Forms of Legacy

1. Accomplishments and the positive impacts they have on others

It is worthwhile to restate that your purpose in life is not about you but about the impact you make, especially on others. Just think about the remarkable things you have around you: educational systems, health institutions, infrastructure, scientific and artistic discoveries, entertainment options, vaccines and drugs, technology, and innovative food breakthroughs. Those are accomplishments made by humans, and they include the legacies of specific people that made contributions and proffered solutions to major challenges in the world. We are all part of economic and social systems that have benefited immensely from the accomplishments of many people. What would you accomplish to create positive impacts for others? Each one of us has something to contribute, and that will form part of our legacies.

2. Personal stories that inspire others to do well for themselves and become agents of change

Living an exemplary life cannot be overemphasized. Being exemplary does not equate to having lots of money or outsmarting all others. It means we are able to let who we are shine through our accomplishments, character, and personal stories. I started this chapter with an important question: What is your story? Now go back to some of the stories we have examined in this book, including that of Ramanujan, Schulze, Schwarzenegger, Klein, Spencer, Fleming, and Alexander. These are stories that inspire us to become better versions of ourselves. Their stories are part of their legacy, and our stories will become part of our legacies. I will discuss this further in the next section.

3. Valuable resources left for others: financial wealth, estates, businesses, et cetera

If you are blessed with material possessions, you can deliberately leave them for specific purposes for use by others after you. America's John D. Rockefeller and Canada's James Armstrong Richardson left substantial resources for the world after them. Although they are classic examples, many people have more than they need. Whatsoever you have can be shared with others. Before you leave, you can even tell the world your wish for how what you leave is to be used, and that will become part of your legacy.

4. Decisions that positively affect others

Our decisions have implications. Anytime you make decisions that affect others, you must think about your legacy. You may be in a position of authority and have influence over others in your family or community, so the decisions you make, whether as an individual or jointly with others, become part of your legacy. Decisions that positively impact others are good legacies.

5. Principles personally lived and then passed on for others to follow to become better people for themselves and society

In your pursuit of personal leadership, you will learn many invaluable principles and acquire priceless experiences. Allowing others to stand on your shoulders and learn from your wealth of experience and the principles you personally lived so they become better people is a good legacy.

6. Being a bridge to directly help others achieve, pull them out of difficulty, provide for their needs, or save them from problems

One of my philosophies in life is that you are most useful to people if you are available when you are most needed. Becoming a bridge for others is also good legacy. When you do for others what they cannot do for themselves or give to others what they cannot repay, you are leaving a quality legacy.

7. Relationships built and maintained with family, friends, and associates

Deep, healthy, cherished relationships cannot be exchanged for material things. They are the most valuable legacies of those who intentionally build them.

As we pursue personal leadership, we must think, plan, and perform good deeds and leave a positive legacy behind. The ultimate result of our lives should be that the world became a better place because we passed through. Next, let's discuss the specific actions to take to leave a memorable legacy.

Leave a Story in People's Hearts

Think about someone you knew in the past. They may be living or not. They could be your former colleague, supervisor, family member, or friend. Choose someone you related with but have lost contact with for whatever reason. What do you remember about the person? If you were to write three sentences about them, what would you write? Do you have a good or bad memory of them?

Now let me give you an example of someone from my own life. During my undergraduate days, I met Professor E. O. B. Ajayi when he taught Thermodynamics and Phase Equilibria. One thing that was clear right from the first day was that this man had a genuine interest in his students' success; he proved to be a conscientious teacher. He had a habit of selecting his final year project students early in the program, sometimes years before final year, so he could personally train them and groom them to become excellent scientists.

I did not fully understand what Professor Ajayi did for my group of six until much later in my life. Once he learned of our keen interest in materials science, he did everything possible to provide the academic support we needed to become successful. Part of that was establishing a new course for the six of us to study microelectronics alongside our counterparts at Massachusetts Institute of Technology (MIT) by corresponding directly with his colleagues there. We used the same curriculum, completed the same assignments, and were tested the same way.

Professor Ajayi's goal was to build our confidence and to set the stage for us to be able to compete anywhere in the world. He coached us through the most difficult subjects in materials science and opened his office door to us to discuss anything career and future related. He carefully worked with each of us to choose our final year projects and ensured that we had all the resources needed to complete our work. He was a mentor, a coach, and a father figure.

After graduation, Professor Ajayi asked each of us what we wanted to do and offered his support in any way he could. Every one of us that ended up attending graduate schools in the US, Canada, Australia, and the UK did so with his recommendation. He also personally told us his story. He had gotten his doctorate in electrical engineering at Stanford University under the supervision of American physicist William Bradford Shockley, the 1956 Nobel Prize winner.

Professor Ajayi returned to his home country of Nigeria in the 1970s, having earned all his degrees in the US, to help to develop other scientists, like my colleagues and me. It is no surprise that his former students now hold important positions all over the world after graduating from reputable schools, including MIT and Stanford. Whenever I remember Professor Ajayi, I remember his selflessness in building the next generation. His story will resonate with me for the rest of my life. I am personally motivated to do the same thing for others.

"Carve your name on hearts, not tombstones. A legacy is etched into the minds of others and the stories they share about you," said Shannon L. Alder. After every funeral, most people leave the graveyard and turn their back, never to return to the tombstone. However, they still remember; they remember the stories. What story will people remember about you? What legacy will you etch in the hearts of others? What will people remember about you? After attaining your life's achievements and successes, will you live on in the hearts of others? How will you leave a story in the hearts of others to remember?

Leave a Direction for People to Follow

Whenever I consider how serious the impact of the direction left by many people in history is upon our existence today, I become cautious of how my legacies will become the direction others will follow. Let me keep this discussion simple. Though not everyone reads books, they all read other people. You could be the book many will read. Your character, values, principles, philosophies, and beliefs form a cardinal part of your legacy. It should not be a surprise that the philosophies, beliefs, and principles of others who lived before us govern our world today.

Greek philosophers shaped the foundation of much of western thought today. Most of what you know and believe about democracy, art, philosophy, drama, and literature today are the legacies of ancient Greek philosophers who took the position that humans need to be curious, seek the truth, look for patterns, and use reason to solve problems.

Your character, values, principles, philosophies, and beliefs form a cardinal part of your legacy.

Socrates was a notable classical philosopher who lived and taught in Athens at a time referred to as the golden age of Greece, circa 400 BCE. His student, Plato, documented his philosophies and later passed them on to Aristotle. Aristotle was the first to document a theory of science.[2]

The works of these great philosophers, including those passed down by Pythagoras on the belief that logic, mathematics, and numbers represent ultimate reality, form the foundation of science, democracy, and socio-political order that we still use today. Most of what we call democracy today is the legacy of Greek philosophers left for us over two thousand years ago.

Over the centuries, we have seen the world being shaped by the thoughts, ideas, beliefs, principles, and philosophies left earlier by others. One of the most profound examples is the spiritual and societal practices exemplified by Jesus Christ, which is still being passionately pursued by billions of people today, even two thousand years later.

My point here is that you and I have the capacity to leave a direction for others to follow in the form of our beliefs, faith, character, values, ideas, philosophies, and principles. One way to be relevant for several generations to come is to leave a code—a positive one—that others can live by. You do not need to be like the great Greek philosophers; there were only a handful of them in history. However, you can leave your faith, good conduct, and examples of your character and positive values for your family and other generations to emulate. You can become the book they will read after you are gone.

Leave a Name for The World to Remember

Think about these names: Winston Churchill, Abraham Lincoln, Mother Teresa, Nelson Mandela, Obafemi Awolowo, Martin Luther King Jr., Mahatma Gandhi, Alexander Bell, George Washington, Ivan Pavlov, and Albert Einstein. What do you remember about each of those names?

Now what about Adolph Hitler, Idi Amin, Vlad the Impaler, Ivan the Terrible, and Saddam Hussein? What do you know or remember about those in the second list? If you are not familiar with all the names in the two lists, I suggest you read about them. The world will remember their names for many centuries to come.

One of the greatest legacies anyone can leave is a name. A good name is better than anything tangible. Our deeds will be associated with our names. Why do you think people protect their names? Why do you think people do not want their names mentioned in certain circles? It because a good name is better than a bad name. Even if a family has spent much over many generations to build a good name, one act of indiscretion by a prominent family member can ruin the family's reputation and destroy the name. Names are sensitive. I care about what people associate with my name, and I hope that you also do. Your name becomes part of your legacy. That legacy depends on what people associate with your name.

Benjamin Disraeli said, "The legacy of heroes is the memory of a great name and the inheritance of a great example." In whatsoever you do, remember that you have a name to protect. We always know you by both your deeds and your name because your deeds and your name are inseparable. If we separate them, then there may be no real identity for you. What will people remember when they mention your name? Remember that a name in itself does not mean much, if anything at all. You give power to your name through your deeds and character.

As you journey through personal achievements and successes in life, you may want to think about how to carve your name in stones of honor, respect, and dignity through what you do. Oh yes, your deeds will speak for you and about you when you have become permanently silent. Your deeds will speak through your name. When the world mentions your name, your deeds will shine. This same idea goes for the names and brands of entities, such as companies, clubs, religious organizations, schools, associations, political parties, et cetera. Leave a name, a good name for the world to remember.

Leave an Inheritance for Generations to Come

One legacy of achievers and people who spend their lives pursuing personal leadership is that they leave physical ways to continue their legacy for generations to come. Many of us have benefited from the benevolence of these great people. These are the successful ones that left a legacy by starting foundations to cater to the needs of the next generation, creating scholarships that send others to school, founding and funding colleges and universities, using their wealth to build hospitals, willing their properties to charities, and leaving properties and businesses to their families.

Know that the success you are seeking will attract many resources to you, including financial resources and other material items. Those who possess both vast financial resources and wisdom know they need much less than they have. If you have spent a significant part of your life gaining much, you could also spend a significant amount of time planning how you would like the world to use those resources after you.

What you leave for others to use and benefit from becomes part of your legacy. In many instances, we refer to material things and money when we talk about inheritance. However, other inheritances may be immaterial. I mentioned a few earlier, including a good name, which your family can also inherit. People can inherit your good will. More importantly, people can inherit your ideas, faith, principles, and philosophies.

Think about the material or immaterial resources you could leave for generations as part of your legacy. Your legacy is important. The seasons of your personal achievements and success will last only as long

Do not let "you" be forgotten. Do today what you would like the world to remember about you tomorrow. Leave a legacy.

as you live. But your legacies will live on. Do not let *you* be forgotten. Do today what you would like the world to remember about you tomorrow. Leave a legacy.

CHAPTER 10 DISCOVERY QUESTIONS

1. Considering the list of seven good legacies in this chapter, and based on your opinion, rank each legacy by ranking them from 1 to 7, where 1 is the most important and 7 is the least important legacy.

2. In two sentences only, what would you like people to remember most about you?

3. List below three personal philosophies you would like to pass on to the next generation. Why do you think your philosophies are important? What are the benefits of your ideas, beliefs, faith, or character to the world?

4. What is the importance of leaving a name to you? Do you currently have a name or a brand you are protecting? How are you doing that?

5. What three material things would you like to leave as inheritances for your family and society? Why is that important to you? Will you share the material things while you are still here, or will you write a will to be executed when you are gone?

CHAPTER 11

WHERE TO GO FROM HERE

Take the first step in faith. You don't have to see the whole staircase, just take the first step.

~ Martin Luther King Jr. ~

Inaction breeds doubt and fear. Action breeds confidence and courage. If you want to conquer fear, do not sit home and think about it. Go out and get busy.

~ Dale Carnegie ~

I conducted a simple search on what people consider the most important things in life. My search returned things such as passion, purpose, goals, family, love, friends, health, education, self-development, hard work, determination, good memories, helping others, time, gratefulness, self-confidence, and happiness. Everyone views the most important things differently. What is most important to you may not be as important to someone else. In addition, factors such as your stage of life, state of mind, past experience, personal views, and lifestyle determine what is most important to you.

Determining what you should focus on achieving at any point as you build your own life's blueprint weighs heavily on your pursuit of personal leadership as has been discussed throughout this book. Every decision or indecision and action or inaction depends on where the individual is on their journey to personal leadership. How we self-examine, self-determine, and take self-responsibility on our journey through life largely dictates the course of our lives. Constant pursuit of personal leadership puts one in a position to deliberately alter the course of their own life.

Where do you want to go from here? Now that you have accessed a rich lode of personal possibilities in this book, it is time to take action. It is time to act on the lessons learned as you continue to grow and develop your capacity for achieving remarkable things. I suggest you use this book methodically by reexamining repeatedly the concepts discussed and taking specific actions with your personal leadership development. Remember that you must take personal responsibility for the direction your life goes and for achieving success in life.

The central theme you should take away with you is that *"The world must make room for a person who has discovered, and has the desire and determination, to develop and exploit their gifts, talents, and abilities to establish themselves in what they have determined to be their exact purpose and calling in life."*

The secret of success and personal achievement is really no secret. However, the collective principles are still a rare gem that must be discovered, analyzed, and practiced by those seeking to know the way to success.

Most appropriate here are the words of Napoleon Hill:[1]

> Everything that has life in this world, with the lone exception of man, comes into life with its life span and its actions and reactions fixed in a definite pattern, through what we call instinct. Man is the only one who comes to life with no fixed pattern, and with the ability to establish and carry out his own pattern, by adapting himself to this great law of cosmic habit force. Yet this law ultimately governs even the thought habits of individuals, which are automatically fixed and made permanent by cosmic habit force, no matter whether they are negative or positive.

The individual creates the pattern of his thoughts by repetition of thought on any given subject. But the law of cosmic habit force takes over these patterns and makes them permanent unless they are broken up by the will of the individual. Man is the only living creature that is equipped with the power to re-arrange these at will.

To alter the pattern of your life, you must first create a thought pattern and repeat that thought pattern until it becomes a habit and the pattern of your life. Constantly be vigilant so only the positive becomes habit, not the negative. Alter the negative actions or thoughts before they can become habit. You have the ability to rearrange these at will. You become what you repeatedly think and do.

It is everyone's responsibility to rise up, shape up, and stand out through the pursuit of personal leadership as discussed in this book. Frank Herbert said, "There is no real ending. It's just the place where you stop the story." This is where I will stop the story, but this is also now the beginning of a journey to great achievements and success for you and for me.

I hope you have been inspired by this book and that you enjoyed every page. I would like to ask you to kindly leave a review or rating wherever you acquired the book or simply go to Amazon, type the book title, and leave a review.

Let us connect.

www.deleola.com | LinkedIn | @TheDeleOla on Twitter & Instagram

BONUS

Inspirational Questions For Personal Reflection

The purpose of the following questions is to help you think through the most fundamental aspects of personal leadership development. Take time to answer the questions as honestly as you can. The questions are not arranged in any particular order.

1. If you were to achieve only one thing in your lifetime, what would that be? Why would you want to achieve it?
2. If money is not a problem and you have all your expenses already catered for, with lots of cash in bank for your future, what would you really like to do as a job, pursue as a career, or do as a business? Is that different from what you are currently doing?
3. When you wake up in the morning, do you feel excited to go to work, or do you wish you had another job, career, or business?
4. Where would you want to be in your career, job, or business five years from now? Can you mention the specific accomplishments you would like to see in your career or business in five years?
5. What are the top five things you really want to do or achieve in your lifetime? How do you think you can achieve them?
6. What do you currently spend most of your time on now? Does that contribute directly to the five things you really want to do?

7. What was the greatest thing you ever achieved or the best performance you gave recently? How did you do it? How did it make you feel?

8. Have you ever had a plan or an idea that you put aside? Why did you put it aside?

9. Is there something you started but abandoned, such as a project, schooling, relationship, journey, et cetera? Why did you stop?

10. Do you find yourself unwilling to share your thoughts with others? What do you think is responsible for your unwillingness?

11. Have you ever been negatively criticized for your suggestion or idea in the past? How did that make you feel? How did you handle the criticism?

12. In what ways are you clearly different from other people around you?

13. How have you assessed your own skills, talents, or natural abilities?

14. Are you aware of a natural talent or gift you have, including physical or intellectual gifts? Could you list them? How did you know you are gifted?

15. Do you have a natural inclination to do certain things very well without much effort? What are they?

16. Is there something you do much better than others? If there is more than one, can you write them down?

17. How often do you try new things, such as new outdoor activities, playing new games, visiting new places, trying new crafts, speaking to new people, reading new books, building new things, et cetera? What new thing did you start recently?

18. Do you find yourself always doing a particular activity daily? Is that what you really want to do, or you just drift

into it? Could that activity be tailored to help you achieve any of the top five things you would like to achieve?

19. Choosing one or two things that you strongly desire to achieve, what practical steps can you take to achieve them? What would you do first? What would you do next? And next? Could you write down five to seven goals/steps to achieve that particular desire?

20. What are the top five values most important to you? Why are they so important? Do you currently keep those values? If not, why not?

21. Looking around you, is there something that you perceive is needed by many people and you have the skill or talent to produce? Is there anything stopping or discouraging you from producing it?

22. Have you ever written down what you will do the next day, the next year, or in five years?

23. Who are the people closest to you right now? Do you think they can support you in achieving what you want to achieve?

24. Who would you work with to achieve your goals and fulfill your desire?

25. What do you plan to do for others? Can you write down how your work, business, or achievements would affect others around you?

26. Why do you want the success you are seeking? When you achieve the level of success you aspire to, what would that mean to you?

27. Thinking about the medium and big choices you made in recent times, did you use any definite process or method for arriving at your decisions? Why or why not?

28. What principles do you use to guide your decisions? For example, when making a financial decision that exceeds

a certain financial value, do you wait a certain period of time, say a day or two, to think before making the decision?

29. What is the most humiliating thing that has ever happened to you? How did you handle the situation? How could you have handled it better? What would you do if you experience a similar situation next time?

30. Do you feel fearful when you are about to do something big? What do you think causes that fear? What could you do to overcome the fear?

31. How do you identify yourself when introducing yourself to others? Why do you introduce yourself that way?

32. How would you describe yourself?

33. Do you think your ethnic background, race, skin color, language, religion, citizenship, or similar social factors have a negative impact on your achievements? In what ways?

34. How did your perspective on your personal identity change after reading chapter one of this book?

35. Could you list four areas of personal strength for you?

36. If you were to change anything about yourself now, what would that be and why?

37. Is there a personal habit you consider unhelpful and you would like to stop? How would you go about stopping it? What good habit could you use to replace the unwanted habit?

38. Is there a good habit you would like to start? What small steps could you take to start?

39. What do you do when things are not within your control but affect you directly or indirectly?

40. If you were given five million dollars today, what would you do with the money?

41. What area of knowledge and skills do you think you are lacking? What could you do to acquire the skills?
42. If you were to write a statement of your life's purpose, what would that be? Could you write it down?
43. What is the most difficult task you have ever completed? How did that make you feel? How did you complete the task?
44. In about five sentences, could you describe the future you would like for yourself in the next five years?
45. What dream did you have as a child? Did you live the dream?
46. When last did you document your ideas? If you do not document your ideas, why not?
47. How did you select your current job, career, or business? How did you determine that you should be doing that? What do you think about your work in relation to chapter five of this book?
48. Do you consider yourself an expert in a particular area of work, field, profession, trade, or business? If not, why not? If so, how did you arrive at becoming an expert?
49. What major distraction do you tend to have while pursuing something important? How can you get rid of the distraction?
50. What is the biggest opportunity you have ever had? How did you use the opportunity? Do you think there is a way you can become visible to more opportunities?
51. Who are the new people you have met in the last year? How did you meet them? What purpose do they serve in your life? What purpose do you serve in their lives?
52. Who did you help recently who might not have been able to help themselves? What help did you render to them?
53. How would you describe your current stage of life?

54. What do you consider the greatest legacy anyone can leave? What would you like your legacy to be?
55. Do you have anyone or a group of people looking up to you? Why do you think they are looking up to you?
56. Are you looking up to anyone as a role model or leader? Why do you look up to them?
57. What is the most important thing to you? Why?

ABOUT THE AUTHOR

Dr. Dele Ola is the award-winning author of *Be a Change Agent: Leadership in a Time of Exponential Change*, publisher of the *Prowezz Leadership Newsletter*, a change leader, and an accomplished professional engineer. His passions include corporate leadership, personal growth, skills development, and technological innovation.

Dr. Ola started his leadership journey with Accenture, a global Fortune 500 company before earning his Doctor of Philosophy in mechanical and manufacturing engineering from the University of Manitoba, eventually transitioning to applied research in aerospace and manufacturing at Red River College Polytechnic. After many significant contributions, he became Director of the Technology Access Centre for Aerospace and Manufacturing, serving as a major contributor to applied research leadership.

Dr. Ola has held many leadership positions and served on the board of several prominent organizations. He won the 2016 Research Excellence BRAVO Award, and his book, *Be a Change Agent*, won the business category of the 2021 Next Generation Indie Book Awards.

An active leader in innovation and applied research, Dr. Ola continues to lead change in his work. His vision is to develop change agents who will challenge the status quo, take charge of the future, and evolve into what they are meant to be in life.

NOTES

Chapter 2. Discover Your Personal Identity

1. Robert C. Jennings, Dr. Seuss: "What am I doing here?" The Saturday Evening Post, February 10, 2016, https://www.saturdayeveningpost.com/2016/02/dr-seuss/
2. Eric T. Olsen, "Personal Identity," *The Stanford Encyclopedia of Philosophy* (Spring 2021), Edward N. Zalta (ed.), https://plato.stanford.edu/archives/spr2021/entries/identity-personal/
3. *Locke on Personal Identity* by Strawson, Galen. 2011, Princeton University Press.
4. "Relative Identity and Locke's Principle of Individuation," in *History of Philosophy Quarterly, 7(3)*, pages 283–297.
5. Isaac Watts, "False Greatness," Preacher Thoughts, Monday, June 15, 2020, http://preacherthoughts.blogspot.com/2020/06/false-greatness-poem-by-isaac-watts.html
6. Stephen R. Covey, *The 7 Habits of Highly Effective People*, Free Press, A Division of Simon & Schuster Inc., Copyright 1989.
7. E. O. Aruma and Melvins Enwuvesi Hanachor, "Abraham Maslow's Hierarchy of Needs and Assessment of Needs in Community Development," *International Journal of Development and Economic Sustainability* 5, no.7: pp.15-27.
8. MP4/4, McLaren, https://www.mclaren.com/racing/heritage/cars/1988-formula-1-mclaren-mp4-4/

Chapter 3. Develop Your Life's Blueprint

1. Jie Jing Chow, "8 Dizzying Facts About Petronas Towers You Probably Did Not Know" Concorde Hotel Blog, Kuala Lumpur, February 2, 2017, https://kualalumpur.concordehotelsresorts.com/8-dizzying-facts-about-petronas-towers-you-probably-didnt-know
2. Petrosains, "World's Tallest Twin Building," Petronas Twin Towers Design & Structure, 2021, https://www.petronastwintowers.com.my/design-and-structures/
3. Lexico, Oxford Dictionary, https://www.lexico.com/definition/desire
4. Napoleon Hill, *Keys to Success: The 17 Principles of Personal Achievement* (Dutton, 1994).
5. "Ecclesiastes 2:11, New Living Translation (NLT), The Futility of Pleasure," BibleGateway, 2015, https://www.biblegateway.com/passage/?search=Ecclesiastes%202&version=NLT

Chapter 4. Cultivate Personal Leadership Attitudes

1. Treehouse Direct, "The Backyardigans: Horsing Around, Ep. 28," December 5, 2014, Video, 24:05, https://www.youtube.com/watch?v=NlHGETgDI90
2. "Horsing Around," The Backyardigans Wiki, https://backyardigans.fandom.com/wiki/Horsing_Around
3. Earl Nightingale on "Winning Attitude," https://www.youtube.com/watch?v=TApxX1Tbo6w&t=29s
4. "Ecclesiastes 10:15, Amplified Bible (AMP), A Little Foolishness," BibleGateway, 2015, https://www.biblegateway.com/passage/?search=Ecclesiastes+10&version=AMP

5. Chaomei Chen, "On the Shoulders of Giants," *Mapping Scientific Frontiers: The Quest for Knowledge Visualization*, 2015: 135-166, https://doi.org/10.1007/978-1-4471-0051-5_5

6. Brian Tracy, *Eat That Frog!: 21 Great Ways to Stop Procrastinating and Get More Done in Less Time*, Berrett-Koehler Publishers, Inc. Copyright 2017.

7. Linda Rodriguez McRobbie, "The Man in the Iron Lung," The Guardian (The Long Read), May 26, 2020. https://www.theguardian.com/society/2020/may/26/last-iron-lung-paul-alexander-polio-coronavirus

Chapter 5. Establish Yourself in Your Life's Work

1. Oliver Hamilton, "The Inspirational Story of Arnold Schwarzenegger's Life," BrainSharper, August 15, 2019, https://brain-sharper.com/entertainment/arnold-schwarzenegger-fb/

2. "Arnold Schwarzenegger," Britannica, up. May 7, 2021, https://www.britannica.com/biography/Arnold-Schwarzenegger

3. "Horst Schulze – Ritz-Carlton Cofounder – Part 1," Faith Collides, January 13, 2020, https://faithcollides.com/horst-schulze/

4. "The History of the Ritz-Carlton Hotel Company," The Ritz-Carlton, accessed July 2, 2021, https://www.ritzcarlton.com/en/about/history

5. "The Ritz-Carlton," Marriot International, accessed July 2, 2021, https://hotel-development.marriott.com/brands/the-ritz-carlton/

Chapter 6. Exploit Your Creative Thinking Ability

1. Steven Tweedie, "How the microwave was invented by a radar engineer who accidentally cooked a candy bar in his pocket," Business Insider, July 3, 2015, https://www.businessinsider.com/how-the-microwave-oven-was-invented-by-accident-2015-4

2. "Discovery and Development of Penicillin: International Historic Chemical Landmarks," ACS Chemistry for Life®, accessed July 1, 2021, http://www.acs.org/content/acs/en/education/whatischemistry/landmarks/flemingpenicillin.html

3. "Sir Alexander Fleming: Biographical," Nobel Prize Outreach AB 2021, accessed Thursday July 1, 2021, https://www.nobelprize.org/prizes/medicine/1945/fleming/biographical/

4. Dick Bourgeois-Doyle, "The Maker: George Klein and the first electric wheelchair," University of Toronto Engineering News, January 25, 2017, https://news.engineering.utoronto.ca/maker-george-klein-first-electric-wheelchair/

5. Clinton Nguyen, "7 world-changing inventions that were ridiculed when they came out," Insider, August 2, 2016, https://www.insider.com/inventions-that-were-ridiculed-2016-8

6. Nick Whigham, "The life changing inventions the experts said were impossible," news.com.au, August 1, 2006. https://www.news.com.au/technology/innovation/inventions/the-life-changing-inventions-the-experts-said-were-impossible/news-story/8c8b0e58532b329d1b6f97c3dfee9fcc

7. Robert Strohmeyer, "The 7 Worst Tech Predictions of All Time," PCWorld, December 31, 2008,

https://www.pcworld.com/article/155984/worst_tech_pre-dictions.html

8. John F. Kennedy Moon Speech – Rice Stadium, September 12, 1962, accessed July 1, 2021, https://er.jsc.nasa.gov/seh/ricetalk.htm

9. "Philippians 4:8, Amplified Bible (AMP), Think of Excellence," BibleGateway, 2015, https://www.biblegateway.com/passage/?search=Philippians%204&version=AMP

Chapter 7. Explore the World of Possibilities

1. "Srinivasa Ramanujan: Indian mathematician," Britannica, https://www.britannica.com/biography/Srinivasa-Ramanujan

2. Robert Kanigel, *The Man Who Knew Infinity: A Life of the Genius Ramanujan*, Washington Square Press, Copyright 1991.

Chapter 8. Understand the Seasons

1. "Ecclesiastes 3:1, New King James Version (NKJV), Everything Has Its Time," 1982, BibleGateway, https://www.biblegateway.com/passage/?search=Ecclesiastes%203%3A1&version=NKJV

2. Stephen J. Mraz, "A Gallery: Boeing 747 Going into Retirement," Machine Design, October 27, 2020, https://www.machinedesign.com/gallery/media-gallery/21146045/a-gallery-boeing-747-going-into-retirement/slideshow

3. "747 COMMERCIAL TRANSPORT/YAL-1: Historical Snapshot," Boeing, 2021, https://www.boeing.com/history/products/747.page

Chapter 9. Become a Role Model

1. Stephen R. Covey, "The Habits of Effective Organizations," in *Leader to Leader: Enduring Insights on Leadership from the Drucker Foundation's Award-Winning Journal*, eds. Frances Hesselbein and Paul M. Cohen (San Francisco: Jossey-Bass, 1999).

2. Dele Ola, *Be a Change Agent: Leadership in a Time of Exponential Change*, FriesenPress, Copyright 2021.

Chapter 10. Leave a Legacy

1. "Proverbs 22:1, Amplified Bible (AMP), On Life and Conduct," 2015, BibleGateway, https://www.biblegateway.com/passage/?search=Proverbs%2022&version=AMP

2. J.P. McEvoy, *A Brief History of the Universe*. (CPI Group (UK) Ltd, 2010).

Chapter 11. Where to Go from Here

1. Napoleon Hill, *Success Habits: Proven Principles for Greater Wealth, Health, and Happiness* (New York: St. Martin's Essentials, 2018).

About Dr. Dele Ola's Award-Winning *Be a Change Agent*

Are you painfully aware of the mismatch between outdated approaches and our rapidly evolving world? Dr. Dele Ola looks unflinchingly at the problem of resisting change and offers a wealth of expert guidance on how to embrace positive growth and foster development.

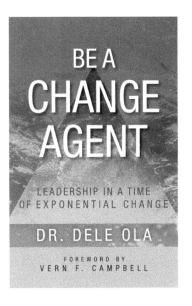

Be A Change Agent is a comprehensive examination of change leadership: the need for it, the qualities of change leaders, and the importance of having great change teams. Dr. Ola first guides the reader through stories of fearless leaders and explores the Veritas qualities that made them successful. Then he discusses building collaborative teams that work well and have the independence to innovate without overt bureaucratic control. Dr. Ola's years working with high-performance teams helped him develop an insightful tool for looking at three spectrums that cause tension in teams:

- The Systems Spectrum-Structure versus influence
- The Reaction Spectrum-Reflection versus action
- The Perspective Spectrum-Reality versus idealism

And the Tensions Equalizer tool will change how you view the balance of members in your team. Finally, the book culminates in a discussion of the future of work, learning, enterprise, and innovation.

Complete with insightful questionnaires and reflection questions, *Be A Change Agent* offers a practical toolkit for both emerging change agents and seasoned influencers to evaluate their leadership qualities and become the very best they can be.

CPSIA information can be obtained
at www.ICGtesting.com
Printed in the USA
LVHW092040020222
710078LV00012B/224/J

9 781777 964504